YOU'RE NOT PRETTY ENOUGH

EXTRAORDINARY STORIES FROM AN (UN) ORDINARY LIFE.

JENNIFER TRESS

For my family.

TABLE OF CONTENTS

AUTHOR'S NOTE

All of the stories contained here are true and based on my memories, as well as the memories of others who were associated with the events. To move the story along, sometimes I truncated timelines or consolidated characters. Some names were also changed.

INTRODUCTION

This is a book about defining moments. We all have them, or a series of them, that when added up give us insight into who we are and why we do things. Come along as I tell you mine…

SEX EDUCATION

When my mom was pregnant with my younger sister, I asked her where babies came from. Being a feminist and a bohemian, she felt obligated to be completely honest. She pulled out a copy of *Our Bodies, Ourselves*—the women's health Bible of that time—and showed me diagrams of reproductive organs and procedures while she narrated.

"When a man's penis becomes aroused, he enters it into a woman's vagina. Once there, sperm is released and travels to the woman's womb. See, this is the womb. An egg is deposited—all women have eggs..."

We have eggs?!

"...If all goes well the sperm from the penis fertilizes the egg, which develops into a baby." She looked down to see me staring at the pictures, riveted.

"Well," she continued, "I guess when a man is aroused he doesn't *always* enter a woman's vagina, but let's save that story, shall we?"

Yes, let's. Because I was four.

My mother says that immediately after this conversation I marched up to my room and emerged two hours later with a collection of pieces that my family now refers to as "The Sex Papers." These works of "art" are sweet, but subversive. Some of them are titled with the word SEX just in case the viewer wasn't sure what the scene was depicting.

Here are two naked people sitting across from each other smiling and smoking cigarettes (note the breasts directly under the chin). I think all the sex scenes in seventies soap operas inspired this—how everyone used to smoke after doing it?

Here's a cheerleader, cheering for sex. Gooooooo SEX! What does the H stand for though? Happy? Horny? Handjobs? Regardless, I obviously felt positively toward it. Sex had to be a good thing if people were cheering about it, right?

2

And who's this comely lady with the strange arms and fashion sense? I'm sure this was my interpretation of 70s fashion, but I don't remember seeing any dresses with holes cut out so that women could properly display their impossibly perky breasts.

This lady is about to have sex with a guy in a beanie and polka-dot pajamas. She appears to be wearing kneepads, which perhaps shows a penchant for rough sex? Maybe that's why the word "SEX" is crossed out?

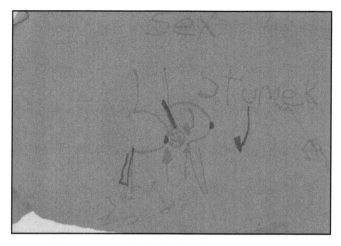

The most technical of all the Sex Papers,
most likely influenced by all those damn diagrams.

Which gave way to the actual baby-making process.
This is how hot pink people make a baby.

Music played constantly in my home: Crosby, Stills, Nash, and Young; Elton John; the Beatles; Stones; Michael Jackson; Donna Summer; and…Marlo Thomas. Yes, I was raised to believe in a land where the horses run free, a land where you and me were free to be, well…you and me. So while clearly SEX took precedence as the overriding theme of the Sex Papers, there were other messages that seeped in. Messages about love, about family, and about being a strong woman. The series concludes with:

"You got to love yourself before you love your baby and your husBENT and when you grow up you get married to your boyfriend or a boy that you love but the important THINE to do is love the whole family." TRUTH.

I quickly moved from my drawing phase to playacting and cast my toys and *Star Wars* action figures in an ongoing production called "Mash Your Privates." This involved me holding two figures—one in each hand—and making them face each other while clacking their plastic torsos together in a savant-like fashion.

These are the pairings that made sense to me:
- Leia and Luke,
- Storm Trooper and Storm Trooper,
- Obi Wan and Yoda,
- C3PO and R2D2,
- Han Solo and Chewbacca, and
- Weeble Wobble and Barbie. Thinking back on this, she must have had a fetish for little people and a goal: but no matter how hard she tried, that Weeble Wobble would. just. not. fall. down. Poor Barbie. Always a bottom.

A path my mom didn't foresee during the "Mash Your Privates" years was plastic doll incest. One day I was mashing the privates of my Donnie and Marie Osmond dolls, and my Mom walked past this scene with a basket full of laundry, and yelled, "For God's sake, Jenny, they're brother and sister!" Then she muttered something incomprehensively and carried the basket upstairs. I paused for a minute—while *Je T'Aime* by Jane Birkin & Serge Gainsbourg played in the background—and looked at their frozen, innocent, smiling faces and their matching pink, purple, and tan outfits. *Well, so are Luke and Leia,* I reasoned, and went back to the mashing.

Of course, none of this had any connection whatsoever with the euphoria that comes from feeling turned on. I didn't know what *that was* until I saw my first Prince video: *Little Red Corvette.* I watched rapt as he batted his Bambi-like eyes and subtly gyrated with the microphone stand, looked right into the camera, and then, my soul.

I didn't quite *get* what this feeling was, but I definitely thought a lot about that tiny androgynous sexpot at night while I wrestled with the sheets.

These wrestling matches started on a random night when I was around thirteen. While I was tossing and turning, the sheet glided between my legs in a very pleasant way and I froze. *What the hell was that?* I thought and proceeded to perform the move fifty-eight more times. So there I was night after night dry humping my bedding.

When *Purple Rain* was released, I went with two friends to the movie theater. We told our parents we were going to see *Gremlins* and bought tickets to that show but snuck into the back of an already darkened theater showing *Purple Rain.* We were not prepared. We gripped our armrests tightly, mouths hanging open as we watched Prince finger-fuck Apollonia and the stars interpret various songs like "Sex Shooter," and "Darling Nikki." It was way too much for our porous minds. What was I thinking jumping from dolls bumping plastic uglies straight to Prince and the Revolution in one move? One should complete that progression in five moves! Minimum! I went home that night completely confused and freaked out yet also excited to "hit the sheets."

"Jenny, are you OK?" my mom asked. "You don't look so good."

"No, fine, just tired. I'm going up to bed."

"How was *Gremlins*?"

I looked directly at her. "Some parts were really, really weird."

That night, amid the sheets, I thought about the scene with Prince and Apollonia. Instead of stopping when I reached that point of near unbearable pleasure—it felt like being tickled—I kept going. *Did I pee?* I wondered and felt the sheets, but nothing was overly wet. For a while, I kept it my own little secret. And took lots of "naps."

My friends and I didn't talk about stuff like that when we were thirteen. And I didn't talk about my own feelings until I knew what they *meant.* I think we realized we knew next to nothing about "grown-up" issues and that we were in that odd, short phase between leaving childhood behind and committing to being teens. We were scared to admit to or share anything that made us look like the weird kid. Unless we knew we weren't alone. I always had respect for the kids who were the first to admit they were cutters or who had bad home lives; you could almost physically see a wave of relief wash over the people who were present for a confession and for an opening to say, "I had no idea. Me too."

This is also the stage in life when most of us had to attend health class, that awful period where you sat through uncomfortable lectures—or in my class, overhead projector diagrams. My junior high health teacher tried to make these lectures fun by doing things like drawing his own overhead slides to guide a particular topic. One that stands out as the most embarrassing was the slide he used to explain the ovulation process by drawing an airplane with an egg jumping out of it yelling, "Ovulaaatttioooon!" as it pulled its parachute ripcord. He did this leisurely while he stood at the front of the class in his white polo shirt and tight, navy blue polyester shorts and raised his hand to simulate the slow, swaying back-and-forth of an object gliding safely to the ground. All he got for his trouble was the sound of silence. Really. You could hear the crickets.

At fourteen my breasts grew from As to bountiful Cs seemingly overnight, which amused my younger sister. Whenever I was being bossy, she retorted by sticking her fists under her T-shirt and stretching the material out to make them look like huge, lopsided breasts and saying, "Whatever!" in the brattiest tone possible. At first I'd lunge, ready to throttle her, but that only seemed to egg her on, so I soon turned the tables. "These puppies?" I'd say, pointing to my chest. "They're comin' for you too." And they did.

This transformation of my chest brought attention mainly from skeevy old men. It later brought on the epiphany that many men are rendered powerless in the presence of big boobs, but at fourteen it only made me uncomfortable, and I tried to hide them under numerous Limited Forenza Shaker Knit sweaters that I color coordinated with my stirrup pants. Sometimes male teachers would call me and other well-endowed girls up to their desks and ask things like, "So, how was your weekend?" while they stretched back in their chairs, arms behind their heads, spreading their legs apart.

Health class ended the same year we completed junior high, and our teacher decided to close out the course with a talent show. It might have made more sense to put on a show with acts relevant to things we learned, like short plays inspired by Madonna's "Papa Don't Preach," but instead it was just a run-of-the-mill talent show. Still in my Prince phase, a friend and I decided we should pair up and do an interpretive dance to "When Doves Cry." We practiced for hours in her screened-in porch, choreographing every last move and settling on show-day outfits of royal blue satin shorts that went down to our mid-thighs, white tank tops, and overly permed hair with lace bows and lots of makeup. We looked like clown boxers.

As we clumsily performed the routine and routinely elbowed each other accidently, our health teacher went from watching us intently to cheering us on for our creativity and heart. I don't remember anyone winning, but upon recalling this with a couple friends from high school recently, I could see one of the girls dusting off the cobwebs in her mind and shouting, "Oh my God, I *SAW* that show." She didn't sound pleased.

At sixteen I started working at a local video store. In the mideighties, Blockbusters had sprung up nearly everywhere, but small towns like mine didn't warrant such an investment. Instead, I worked at a store called Stop N' Go Video, which was about seven hundred square feet and located in a strip mall. After I got the initial and brief training, I worked my shifts alone and was responsible for closing out the cash register and securing the store. Often, my friends would visit, and we'd watch movies that were PG enough to withstand any potential customer's taste meter. Booooorrrring.

At least, that was until we discovered a system for the porn. We didn't have enough space for a back room to store the X-rated box covers, so Stop N' Go's solution was to create a binder with either the video boxes flattened in the laminate sleeves or the promotional fliers from the distribution companies. Patrons would have to come to the front counter and ask for "the binder" to flip through and make their selection, which was located under the cash register.

This created countless embarrassing situations where the customer was forced to peruse such titles as *Anal Annie and Magic Dildo* or *Whore of the Worlds* at the front desk while I diverted my attention to *anything* else, such as furiously cleaning the phone. Many times, parents of friends or even teachers would enter the store, see it was me working, spend some time looking through the "family" genre row, and then turn to me and say, "Looks like I've seen everything, Jen!" before walking out. Mmm hmm. See you next time.

I also encountered several boys, some as young as thirteen, trying to rent the tapes. I'd humor them and ask for their IDs, and they'd make up some lame excuse. But every once in a while, if I knew they were at least fifteen and terribly bookish, I'd let them flip through the binder first before asking for identification. In those rare instances, I felt justified that by giving them what I was sure was an infrequent glimpse at a naked woman, I was somehow better preparing them to deal with the fairer sex in the future. Relax. I didn't grow up to be a child psychologist.

My girlfriend Nikki and I, however, were the biggest viewers of the porn. Curious after giggling over the binder ourselves, we graduated to viewing movies in the store's VCR later at night. We learned about moves and positions in that video store by viewing the tapes and asking each other questions to clarify our understanding. "Ew! Are we supposed to *like* that when we get older?" I asked after viewing a particularly messy escapade. "Do you do that with Dan?"

"The Pearl Necklace? No! God, *gross!*" she'd say as she rewound the scene for the sixteenth time.

I'd try out expressions and inflections I learned, purring porn phrases at odd times to my high school boyfriend: "Yeah, you like that, don't you?" I'd ask as I kissed him. "You're a bad, bad boy." He'd look at me strangely. "Uh, yeah, I guess so," and we'd continue to make out with me thinking all the while that the scenario would be even sexier if the pizza delivery guy showed up.

Viewing and studying women in porn became the template for what I assumed men perceived as desirable: arched backs, slightly parted mouths, and closed-eyed moans. The fact that I'd been schooled in this area by Nina Hartley and Tracy Lords may have been undetectable by mere mortal high school boys, but it gave me that extra swagger—something I knew would be uncorked with the right partner who respected all the parts of me...someday.

Which was not the case with my first time. When I was a sophomore, I had an unrequited crush on a senior who ran with the popular crowd but had an outsider's depth to him. He rarely talked to me, but some of his friends dated some of my friends, so we'd see each other at parties on the weekends, where he drank a lot and went upstairs with numerous girls.

He was thickly built, tall and muscular, and wore tight tank tops under flannel shirts. He had dark, slightly curly hair, large hazel eyes, lush lips, and face stubble that got heavier as the day wore on. He commanded drinking games and made people laugh. But he also looked melancholy and far away sometimes. He seemed to me a boy who needed saving. And I thought he saw something special in me too. When I entered a room, he would look at me, without smiling, for ten whole seconds, and I would return the gaze until he broke it. He always broke it first. I thought we were communicating something in a secret code that only we could understand and that all of it meant passion and love.

At one of these parties, he asked me what I was doing after school on a Tuesday.

"Nothing."

"Want to hang out at my house?"

"Yeah, sure."

"Cool."

"Cool."

I told my mom that I was volunteering to decorate the basketball team's lockers and met him in the parking lot after school. We went to his place and drank some of whatever his parents had the most of in their liquor cabinet—I think it was vodka—and watched TV for about an hour. Then he stood up, grabbed my hand, and led me to his bedroom, which was small, sparsely decorated, and contained two twin beds. He laid me down on one of them and immediately got on top of me and began to kiss me and press his crotch roughly down on mine.

A real-life game of Mash Your Privates!

He grabbed my hands with his and raised them over my head.

This is happening! I thought to myself. *Oh my God, this is happening?!*

Yes! Calm down.

He tugged at my shirt and raised it over my head and tossed it on the floor. Then he took his shirt off and laid back down on me and we continued to kiss. A minute later he leaned back and said in a quiet voice, "Take your pants off."

I did as commanded while he put on a condom and then lay on top of me and entered. I was so "in the moment" that I couldn't even recall my porn training. I stared over his shoulder up at the ceiling, wincing a bit in pain and wondering when the "feel good" part was going to happen. *But still,* I thought, *it's with him.* And in a few minutes it was over. He got off me, looked down at a small dark red spot, and asked whether I needed a towel, and I looked down and saw that I did. He started to get dressed and so I followed suit, and then he said, "I should probably take you home; my mom'll be here soon."

"OK, cool."

He drove me back to my neighborhood but dropped me off about a quarter of a mile from my house and said, "You can walk from here, right?"

"Of course I can," my MO at that time being to have a stiff upper lip and project an air of not giving a shit, whether or not it was true. But that late afternoon I thought that was just the way these interactions went.

"Thanks so much for the ride."

I got out of the car feeling at the time like I was different. *I'm a woman now,* I thought. I entered my house and drifted past my mom, who was cooking dinner, and into my sister's room, where she was playing with her toys. "Well, hello, young lady," I said to her. "Did you finish your homework?"

"Did *YOU?*"

The next day at school, he hardly even talked to me. The only acknowledgement was a head tilt as he passed me in the hall and a monotone, "What's up?" *What's up? I just gifted you with my virginity is what's UP. Doesn't that at least deserve a walk to my next class or a sharing of a cigarette out by the football field, asshole?* That's what I wanted to say, but instead I returned the head tilt, said "Not much," and ducked into the nearest bathroom to cry. It sucked to know I was used. Especially when that realization was the polar opposite of the fantasy I had constructed.

Looking back I believe those soulful stares were merely tacit recognition that for him I was a sure thing. The only truly remarkable part about the experience was that he didn't care.

A few weeks after this, my mom took me for my annual checkup with the doctor, who was also my pediatrician from way back. She explained that this appointment was going to be a little different than the others—that this one was going to be more of the gynecological nature.

I took all of this in and thought, *OK, so the guy who's examined me since I was a baby is now going to be sticking his fingers in my vagina. OK.* And then: *Oh God, he's going to know I'm not a virgin anymore! He's going to stick his hands in my vagina and immediately feel that my hymen is broken and then gasp and pull out his hand in shock and look at my mom.*

"What?" she'll ask, startled.

"Your daughter," I imagined him saying, "is no longer your sweet little angel." And my mom will look at me and cry a single, disappointed tear like that Indian in the seventies anti-litter ad campaign who saw you throwing your trash on the freeway.

"Mom, I'm not a virgin!" I screamed, and my mother slammed on the breaks amid angry honks and pulled over to the side of the road.

"What? Who? When? Are you sure? Are you OK? Do you want to talk about it? Who?"

"Mom, it was a boy at school," I said, crying. "He doesn't like me. It was only once. And I will NEVER, EVER do it again!" My mom hugged me and stroked my hair. "He wouldn't have been able to tell," she said, referring to my pediatrician.

That night she tucked me in. The doctor had given me a serious STD talk, which grossed me out but also stayed with me. "You know what sucks about AIDS?" I posed. "You can't just go out there and have a one-night stand anymore."

"One-night stands aren't all they are cracked up to be," she responded and gave me a look like she knew from experience.

A few months later, another boy and I were sexually active and exclusive throughout the remainder of my high school experience. Lucky for me, that boy built the bridge between being treated poorly by a partner and being treated kindly and gently. He wasn't afraid of my burgeoning sexuality, or jealous. He didn't push or force if I didn't want to fool around.

I'm grateful to him for that early imprint on my brain. But, the sex was still…high school sex. It wasn't until twenty-seven or twenty-eight that I had that "I'll have what she's having" moment (I know, I know: *what the fuck, right?*) and I'm grateful for that as well, because once you have *that experience*, you can never go back.

And thank God for that.

CONTRA DANCING AND THE ART OF TEENAGE REBELLION

My sole act of teenage rebellion was going to church. Adult rebellion? That's a few chapters ahead. But teenage rebellion? Not so much. Sure, I drank some in high school and dabbled in psychedelics, but I was a good student, came home by curfew, and rarely got in trouble.

My mom is an atheist and my dad is agnostic. They came by it honestly. My mom grew up Protestant, attending church regularly with her mother and sister. In her late teens, she thought, *You know what? I don't buy it.* So she stopped going, and finally my Nana stopped pushing. My Dad is Jewish. Soon after he became bar mitzvah his mother died of cancer and his visits to temple slowed. His small congregation was populated mainly with people sixty and over, so it wasn't very engaging for a fourteen-year-old grieving boy. My grandfather Abe didn't push either.

I came by my teenage spiritual state dishonestly, I felt. I was non-spiritual by proxy. My parents, on the other hand, had something to *reject.* Still, there was something missing for them in the early seventies. They were looking for like-minded people, for fellowship. And they found it at a Unitarian Universalist church. Unitarian Universalism is similar to what we "modern spiritualists" refer to as *The Universe*, meaning it's all-inclusive and super vague.

"I got a sign from the Universe today!"

"What was it?"

"An e-mail alert telling me those boots I want are on sale!"

In the seventies our church attracted a friendly, middle-class liberal community—people who had and continue to have beliefs such as "free and responsible search for truth and meaning" and "respect for the interdependent web of all existence of which we are all a part." I loved it there. Each Sunday I looked forward to approaching the grounds, which one would begin to see from two miles away— green, velvety, short-cut hilly grounds in the warm months and bright orange, red, and pink leafy trees until winter. I mean, you can imagine the egg hunts. Atop the tallest hill stood the physical dwelling, which was shipped from England and reassembled: a grand Tudor-style home that housed numerous rooms, a kitchen, and a large space with huge, knotted oak beams and hardwood floors for the sermons and dances.

My parents made friends there, and my sister and I made friends with their children. On Sundays I went to classes with other young children, while the older kids and adults went to the sermon. Most of the class lessons came from the Bible and were selected for their entertainment value, to get us to focus. Sometimes we'd act them out; sometimes we'd finger paint. I remember we held an impromptu production of the story of Joseph (son of Jacob) complete with props and costumes from the storage closet in our playroom. Joseph connects the stories of Abraham, Isaac, and Jacob to the freeing of the Israelites in Egypt. He also had that sweet Technicolor dreamcoat.

After class we'd go down for refreshments and play and play and play while our parents socialized. On weekends sometimes they'd hold Contra dances, and the whole family would come. The kids would watch or jiggle on the sides as our parents skipped through partnered folk dances in two lines facing each other. Sometimes there would be costumes and sometimes, as we got older, we kids got to try it too. It was exhilarating.

After my parents divorced, my younger sister and I moved with my mom to a new town about thirty miles away, so we stopped attending. I missed it. My dad moved to an apartment about thirty miles away too—both from the church and from us. Alas, the religious aspects didn't stick. Religion just didn't seem fun. But that church? *That* was fun.

It wasn't until I was about fourteen that I noticed my friends were doing things and talking about things that I wasn't doing or talking about. *The horror!* My only thoughts on religion were abstract. So I started asking my friends questions about their respective faiths, and they invited me to tag along.

"Mom," I declared one night after school, "I'm going to church."

"Okkkaaaayyy," she said. "Which one?"

"All of them."

"Okaaayyy. Well, how did this come about?"

"Well, all my friends go to church with their families on Sundays and they all see each other there, and I just want to find out about God, and you guys think you're so cool because you had that growing up, but then you said, 'no thanks,' but you never gave *me* the chance to say 'no thanks,' so actually that's not very cool at all."

My mother snickered but tried to conceal it.

"OK," she said. "Just don't expect a ride."

My father agreed as well (he married two independent shiksas, incidentally), and for a little while I studied up on Judaism and talked to rabbis, but it was the historical elements that fascinated me most, not so much the dedication ceremonies. I had a friend who was from the Church of Jesus Christ of Latter Day Saints, and he brought me to some gatherings. I disliked the missionary aspect (I *do* like the position), however, and soon moved onto Christianity. In the most general terms, the Lutherans seemed the most laid back and socially aware and the Catholics the most unbending. Perhaps it was the particular priest in my small town's Catholic church, Father Lee. He was cold and technical and boomed when he should have lilted.

When I was in my junior year, my friend Tina's thirteen-year-old brother accidentally shot himself. Me and my group of friends were grief-struck and circled around the family. At the funeral Father Lee spent seemingly endless amounts of time saying,

"He will never play football!"

"He will never see his sisters get married!"

"He will never go to prom!"

"He will never fall in love!"

I looked over at my friend and put my hands over my ears and then looked over at his mother who was sobbing. A few years later, at the rehearsal for my same friend's wedding, Father Lee pre-chastised us about taking Communion.

"Do NOT eat a wafer or take a sip of wine if you are not Catholic. This is the body of Christ! This is the BLOOD OF CHRIST! Do NOT reach for either of these if you are..."

"Yeah, we got it, Father," one of the groomsman said. We all shuffled uncomfortably, and I remember thinking, *why don't you explain the symbolism in a way that draws us in? Makes us think?*

"Well, you had better."

Really, though, I was lazy. I've never fully read the Bible or the Torah. And I have barely scratched the surface on the Muslim faith or Buddhism. Before I finished high school, I ended my quest (via organized religion, anyway). My parents asked me questions, and I'd give them my evolving thoughts while they nodded in encouragement and let me get to the answers on my own.

Where I landed is where I still am today. I like the admittedly simple idea of a God sitting above watching over us, letting us be ourselves, and making decisions that are best for our own personal circumstances as long as we follow The Golden Rule. If we don't, God steps in and removes the bad element, be it weather, for example, or human. And if God doesn't remove it, then there is a lesson to be gained or an epiphany or another path to take. And from there, we would *learn* those lessons and implement change for the better. But that's not reality. It is hard and scary to imagine what is coming around the corner. It sometimes feels like the proverbial finger is on an increasingly pressurized stream coming through a hole in the dyke. But when there is hope—and somewhere there always is—that is because it comes from within us or is inspired by what is around us here on the ground.

HOW TO BE RESPONSIBLE

I knew pretty early that I liked material things and that if I wanted them, I'd need to make my own money, so at twelve I started baby-sitting. Besides a few odd jobs here and there I babysat consistently for one family only: our next-door neighbors, the Cooks. Mac Cook was a tall, lanky mechanic. He was also the president of the Sly Fox Motorcycle Club, so he seemed like a badass, but he had gentle eyes and reminded me so much of Jim Croce that I couldn't help but hum "Bad, Bad Leroy Brown" when I saw him. His wife Leslie was a barfly pixie. She was tiny and pretty—just over five feet and just under one hundred pounds—and sported frosted, perfectly feathered hair that came to her shoulders. She had an easy demeanor and a voice that sounded like she smoked and drank every Friday night, which she did. They both did. We liked them.

They had a tow-headed two-year-old son named Cody who was all giggles and curiosity. I sat for them when they went to the local neighborhood bar, PC's, which has since burned down but remained for years as a charred homage to crushed dreams. Cody and I filled our evenings performing typical babysitter/kid activities: making cookies, watching TV, and me trying to convince him he was really tired and that *it's time to go to bed now.*

We also invented a game that, looking back, I suppose spoke to the more dominant/ submissive sides of our respective personalities. It was simple, and it involved me continuously tripping him. I'd take the cushions from the sofas and pile them on either ends of the living room. Cody would start at one end and gather up as much speed as one could with stubby legs in a fourteen-foot length space and run toward the other end of the room. I'd stick my foot out at the appropriate time, which would trip him and send him face first into the pillows. He'd always shoot up, giggling profusely and demand "Again!" Sometimes the giggling would start before my foot even shot out, the anticipation nearly toppling him on its own. We'd do this for at least an hour, and once we'd get our rhythm my foot would take on a life of its own, instinctively knowing when to shoot out as I watched TV.

After I put him to bed, it was time to wait for the *return of Leslie.* Being tiny, her alcohol tolerance was low, so she always returned home earlier than her husband and *highly* intoxicated. The first time I babysat for the Cooks it was around eight when I heard Leslie stumbling up the steps. After a couple failed attempts to unlock the front door, I got up and opened it.

"Hi doll!" she beamed. "Thanks. These keys don't open shit!"

I looked down and saw she was jiggling the slack part of her metal belt.

"What'd you guys do?" she slurred as she fell back on the couch, and then, "Ooooh cookies! Can I have one?" I brought her the plate, and she took one and winked at me. "This one looks perfect."

Not knowing the protocol for getting paid for an honest night's work but feeling it was important that I got my money before I left the house, I waited for her to hand me some cash. Instead we sat and watched *The Dukes of Hazzard* at opposite ends of the couch for a while until I got up to go to the bathroom and plan my exit. When I returned, Leslie was passed out, nearly horizontal, and her right breast had popped out of the tan suede vest that was the only piece of clothing she wore on the top half of her body. I just stared at the small orb, not knowing what to do.

Do I try and push her boob back in? I asked myself.

Are you kidding? This is above our pay grade; call Mom!

When she walked into the house, she took in Leslie, who was in the exact same state. Then she looked at me, and seeing that I was all wide-eyed, she let out a little laugh, which made me laugh. "Leslie," Mom called out. Nothing. "Leslie," my Mom said again, this time nudging her gently. The orb shook.

"Uhhn, huh?" she responded.

"Leslie, I'm going to make some coffee." Leslie swatted at the air breezily, as if signaling that she was just fine the way she was.

My mom brought the coffee to Leslie and propped her up so that she could drink it. Her breast thankfully slid back into its hiding place. "Thanks, hon," Leslie said, rubbing her eyes and wrapping her hands around the mug. Mom sent me back home because my sister was alone and followed a little while later, with my ten dollars for services rendered.

Another time after I put Cody to bed, the phone rang, and I picked it up to hear my mom on the other end.

"Look out the front window."

I pulled the phone with me and peered out. The Cooks lived at the top of a fairly long driveway, and at the bottom I could see a figure wobbling around on all fours.

"Is that *Leslie?*" I asked.

"Yep," my mom said. "That's Leslie, the all-terrain vehicle."

"Wow. Should we help her?"

"No." Then she followed up with a phrase that is probably the first time I remember irony staring me straight in the face: "She hates to be embarrassed."

We watched her make the slow crawl up the driveway, together on the phone. Every so often she'd stop and put the jacket she was holding on the ground and lay down.

"Is she taking a *nap*?" I asked.

"Looks that way."

"I'll make the coffee," I said.

I was making a lot of coffee in those days—and not just for the Cooks.

INSECTS AND OTHER SUCH SNACKS

My parents divorced when I was seven. Divorce is disorienting, especially for kids. Suddenly we went from one house to two and from two parents to four as both my mom and dad remarried. My dad was climbing up the corporate ladder and soon had a nice new house where we had great clothes and toys, but we had to keep them there. My mom wasn't making a lot of money in those days, and so we didn't have those things at her house and had to go on food stamps for a while. It was confusing at times.

As a kid, I attended a Unitarian church with my family. When my parents separated, they must have arranged who would go as a means to avoid each other because I don't remember seeing them there at the same time again. One day in the children's class, when I was around six, I was asked to light a candle and burned my finger in the process. Later, we all congregated in the main communal area where the church served refreshments. I sat sulking in a corner while the other children played, with my finger wrapped in a cold, wet cloth and elevated on the table. A man approached me. He had slightly long, curly brown hair and wore a funky shirt with a navy blue corduroy blazer and jeans. He asked what happened, but I didn't say anything, so he kneeled down to my level.

"I have a daughter," he said. "She kind of looks like you." He nodded toward my hand and smiled at me. "Can I take a look?"

I gave him my hand. "What's her name?" I asked.

"Jules," he said and unwrapped the cloth. "You know what helps?" I shook my head no. "If you wet it and blow on it." I watched as he dabbed my finger on the wet cloth and told me to do just that. He was right.

"Hello?" my mom said as she knelt down beside us and grabbed my knee. "I'm Jenny's mom, Cathy. I haven't seen you here before." She wore her hair long in those days and was dressed in a flouncy skirt and a light blue knit sweater with no bra. He noticed.

"I'm a new member," he replied and smiled. They started to chat and then slowly stood up. "Keep blowing on that finger, Jenny," he said, and I watched them talk and flirt while I kicked my stocking legs under the chair. They married a couple years later.

We lived in a neighborhood that was poor and was made up of summer cottages—situated around a lake—that were converted into permanent residences. As I grew older, I grew more embarrassed about where we lived. From far away, it was beatific and peaceful, but when I became a teenager, I became hyperaware of how appearances from all aspects of one's life translate into "who you are" and how people view you. In junior high, I'd hear people talking either directly or indirectly about my neighborhood, and despite the status it achieved by housing a couple of popular kids, I was left with the clear impression that my community was the proverbial other side of the tracks. And this was in a town where the tracks were pretty modest to begin with.

When I viewed my neighborhood through that lens, several descriptors came to mind: run-down, deadbeat, poor. This was not how I wanted people to see me, so I distanced myself from the tiny houses where the paint and the siding were stripping away; I distanced myself from the lawns littered with debris and cars or trucks and the people who proudly sported mullets and openly drank alcohol while walking the loop around the lake in naturally faded jeans.

*My mom calls this my "Prom Queen of the
Appalachia" look (though I was not Prom Queen).
Note our house's serious need for a paint job
and the chicken coop in the back.*

Still, we had woods and that private lake and a beach, and we
fished and swam and played outside for as long as the weather
would let us. We also had a big garden and tons of animals—
chickens, dogs, cats—lots and lots of cats, which brought with
them an army of fleas. My sister and I loved the cats. We hated
the fleas (*really? So surprising!*). At the time we shared a room,
and when we'd enter it, we'd watch as they'd land on our legs in
a rush.

But there was a bigger parasite in the house, and that was my stepfather Richard. He saw the flea situation not so much as a nuisance

or even a health hazard; he viewed it more as a learning opportunity. And that's because he was an entomologist, so he looked for any opportunity to teach my sister and me about insects. The fleas especially loved white socks, and when we'd wear them, they would cling to us faster, in more volume, and stay longer. My stepfather would give us glasses of soapy water, which killed them immediately. We'd sit on the floor, pluck them off, and watch them float to the bottom and drown.

There were other teachings about insects. Randomly, he'd launch drills that required my sister and me to go outside and collect bugs. We'd pin them on corkboards, and he'd help us identify them by the unique tapestry of their shells and wings. We sort of liked that. We did *not* like his other attempts to gain our interest on the topic, though, including cooking larvae, crickets, and other insects *for us to snack on,* saying that Americans are in the cultural minority by not including insects in their food pyramid.

"Um, yeah, no thanks," I'd say. "I used my food stamp allowance to buy this bag of Yodels, so I'm all set."

When we first met Richard, he was cool, open, playful—more of a friend. After he and my mom married, he was home with my sister and me a lot after school. My mom worked full time (often overtime) at a hotel down the street. Richard worked only sporadically as a beekeeper inspector, testing Northern Ohio hives for Foul Brood disease. He was incredibly smart—early on in his career he discovered a beetle. He became the preeminent scholar and professor on said beetle, which led to numerous articles in prestigious beetle-related publications. So, it wasn't like he couldn't *get* work, it's just that he would only work when he was sober, which wasn't often. He rested, intoxicated, on his beetle-related laurels.

This mix of smarts, oddness, and drunkenness created the perfect storm of creativity when doling out punishments. For instance, we used to keep cat food in the oven to prevent all our cats from scratching open the bags. I used the oven a lot to heat up snacks after school for my sister and me, and almost always, I forgot the cat food was in there. Soon the smell of burnt Meow Mix would waft throughout the house. Yelling didn't work, nor did sending me to my room. What worked was one day Richard saying to me that if I was so fond of wasting cat food then perhaps I should just eat it. You know, kill two birds with one stone.

"Eat the cat food?" I asked.

"That's what I said."

"How am I supposed do that?"

He went to the cupboard and pulled out a bowl and then a spoon and set it on the table in front of me. He then grabbed the burnt cat food from out of the oven and poured it into the bowl and then took some milk out of the fridge and poured it on top of the cat food. "That's how." He leaned against the kitchen counter, crossed his arms, and watched. This made me feel like I was in the midst of a battle of the wits (and I wanted to win). I'm a rebel from way back. It's literally in my blood (see photo on next page).

So I did what any nine-year-old rebel would do: I ate the cat food, which had the texture and shape of Lucky Charms cereal and tasted like burnt, salty toast. "Mmmmm," I said, looking at my stepfather. "This is the best meal I ever had!" Richard stormed out of the room and slammed his bedroom door. I took the bowl of cat food and threw it away in the woods.

My great-grandfather, William, second from right, with his cousins Emmett and Bob Dalton from the infamous Dalton Gang. The Dalton Gang was a gang of brothers who operated as bank and train robbers/outlaws from 1890–1892. They were also related to the Younger brothers who rode with Jesse James.

At night, Richard would goad my Mom into partying. One night I remember them playing "Another One Bites the Dust" by Queen over and over until I yelled, "Can you please keep it down? *SOME* of us have to get up in the morning!" Then they'd giggle and go into their bedroom, where they'd drink some more and eventually fight and slam doors. Richard was a mean drunk. Critical. And so bitter about his own divorce that my mom often pointed out to him, "You know you hate your ex-wife more than you love me?"

When I officially became a teenager, my mom got a job as an account manager at an advertising agency in Cleveland. She had ten dollars in her checking account. Richard wasn't contributing much financially, but she immediately took us off the food stamp program as a symbolic measure and stopped drinking as a literal one. She felt she was at a crossroads and decided to take the more serious path. Richard wasn't pleased to lose his drinking buddy and frequently left the house at night.

Soon after I entered eighth grade, I became BOY CRAZY. So when the boy I had *the most massive crush on* asked if I would be at the football game that Friday I said "Yes!" louder than necessary. I was obligated to babysit for our next-door neighbors, the Cooks—as I did almost every Friday night—but procrastinated in telling them.

A massive snowstorm hit the area the same week, which was not unusual from October through April in northeast Ohio. What was also not unusual was the "life must go on" sentiment of my people when it came to the weather. This meant that the high school football game would go on as scheduled, and this also meant that the Cooks would be looking forward to slinging back Jack Daniels by 5:30 p.m. at the bar down the street.

By Friday after school, I knew the clock had run out. I needed to get permission to go to the game, but in doing so I would reveal I was shirking my responsibilities with the Cooks. My mom was still at work, so I had to clear it with Richard. *Dammit!* I told him that I wanted go to the game more than anything and, anticipating his protest, threw in a "and I need to experience life for once!" statement. I could see the wheels turning in his mind.

"Sure," he said. "Go right on over and let them know."

"Really?" *It was that easy?*

"Yep. Go right on over. Just go over in your bare feet."

Ah…there it is. "But there's snow on the ground."

"So?"

"So, I'll catch a cold!"

"Well, you wanted to experience life for once."

For reasons I still don't understand, I determined it was whacked but inarguable logic and set out immediately before he changed his mind. The snow crunched when I stepped into it and went up to my mid-calf, so I ran in quick steps to ward off the cold and numbness. I knocked on my neighbor's door, and Mr. Cook opened it.

"I have to go to the football game because Mike just broke up with Kim and she is really upset, but she doesn't want to tell her parents, and so she really needs to be out of the house, and I am the only person she will talk to, and Richard said I could go as long as I came over in my bare feet and told you and you didn't care!"

Mac looked at my bare shins and feet and smiled at me kindly, but his eyes were sad. "Well, I'm bummed you didn't tell me earlier man, but OK."

"OK, thanks!" I said and turned to trounce back.

"Hey!" Mac called after me. I turned to look back at him, shivering.

"Tell Richard he's an asshole and that I will kick his ass if he makes you do something like…" and then he waved his hand angrily at my legs.

"OK!" I called and turned back toward the house.

"What did he say?" Richard asked.

"That I could go."

And that was that. No big lesson.

My mom and Richard divorced that same year. It was weird to see him go, but I didn't feel particularly attached. On the day he left, I was outside reading a book in the grass, leaning up against a tree. He came over and knelt down to my level, just like when I was a little kid with the burned finger at church.

"I'm leaving," he said. "Keep your studies up. You're smart."

"OK...bye."

I never saw him again—never heard from him. But I still remain fascinated by bees.

SHOT THROUGH THE HEART

I dropped my book and stared at the TV. It was late fall 1986, and I was at my dad's house for the weekend, half-watching MTV loop its most popular videos. But this one I hadn't seen before. *Who is this band? Who's that **guy**?*

The video itself was kind of average—just some glorified concert footage with typical hair-band aesthetics: skin-tight leather pants; adoring groupies wearing heavy makeup; lame pyrotechnics; and big, teased hair.

But who is that *guy*? What I remember most about him is his beautiful, sculpted face—the face that launched a thousand of my daydreams. He bounced around the stage playfully, smiling big and sweet. He was sexy, but not overtly sexual. He was different from the other singers in that genre who looked like they would either screw you or kill you before stealing your eyeliner and Aqua Net.

I made sure I didn't blink toward the end of the video when they showed the band's name at the bottom left corner of the screen.

"DAD!" I yelled. "We need to go the drugstore so I can get some magazines!"

"Right now?"

"Yes, right now!"

I bought every *Teen Beat* and *Tiger Beat* I could get my hands on and clutched them carefully until we got home. From then on, I digested every last detail about Jon: Born in New Jersey on March 2, 1962. *That's only an eight-year age gap, reasonable.* Started sweeping floors in a recording studio at seventeen. *Doesn't mind doing menial tasks to further his dreams, so he's a hard worker and not stuck up.* Released his first song, "Runaway" in 1983.

Proving I was the best Bon Jovi fan.

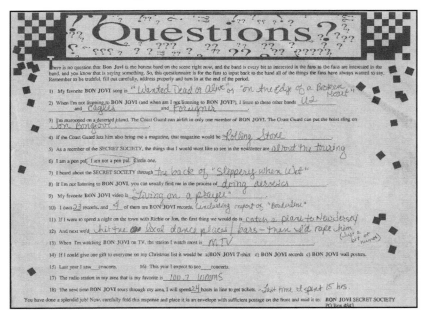

People say I became obsessed, but I say I became passionate and focused. I used my allowance to buy magazines, records, cassettes, and VHS tapes to record videos. I made scrapbooks and hung posters in my room. I slowly transitioned my style from loose-fitting clothes in soft Easter-colored pastels to tight, torn, acid-washed jeans and bolder, sexier colors like red and black.

I am follicly blessed.

After school I watched my little sister until our mom arrived in the evening. Delaying homework, I'd hold the TV hostage watching Bon Jovi videos, pausing the frame every time a close-up of Jon came on the screen and then advancing slowly to study every nuance of that perfect face. Day after day, I'd let my mind wander into a dream world where I was Jon's girlfriend. He'd invite me on tour, and I'd watch each concert from just offstage, where he'd turn from the spotlight and sing the most piercing lyrics directly to me. At night we'd forgo partying with the band to watch *The Golden Girls* and eat room service on our hotel room's king-size bed.

I was barely sixteen and in my sophomore year. Though I still had hormonal urges—including many middle school masturbatory fantasies starring Prince—none could compete with the force of that first big crush. I didn't get asked out on many dates—but I did get asked to school dances. During the "Year of Jon," I'd politely decline, saying my parents wouldn't let me date until I was a junior. I'd tell this to my mom, thinking I was being clever.

"But, honey, you know I'd let you go to dances."

"I know. I'm just saving myself."

"For who?"

"For Jon!"

"OK…but until, you know, that *happens,* you should still have fun."

"Oh, OK," I'd say, rolling my eyes. *These are just boys,* I'd think about the kids in my high school. *Jon is a man.*

My mom glanced at me sideways, looking like she was filing this moment under, "Is my kid crazy?"

Though I was certain I was the only one who truly *understood* Jon, I was self-aware enough to know that others liked him too. When Bon Jovi announced their *Slippery When Wet* tour dates, two friends and I strategized on the best place to camp out for tickets. Our plan required waiting in line overnight at the mall, and my mom was not immediately onboard, but I wore her down.

"Pleasepleasepleasepleasepleasepleasepleasepleaseplease-pleaseplease?" I said, face scrunched in pain, hands clenched, and arms stiffly by my side as if I'd freeze that way if she said no.

"I don't know…"

"Mom, the Mentor Mall is across the street from Margie's, so if anything goes wrong, I can just go there. PleasepleasePLEASE?" Margie was my mom's friend, so it was tough for her to say no.

"Geez, OK. Just…relax."

"Thank you," I said, hugging her tightly. "Everything will be fine, promise!"

It was snowing on the evening we were to set out, and our parents protested lightly, but once that permission is granted, teenagers would rather go through hell than give it back. So, off we went: Jill and Diane and me.

We didn't even make it out of Newbury, Ohio, our small hometown.

On Route 87, two miles from my house, we hit an icy patch of road. We spun sideways and wound up half in the road and half in a field next to Skip's Tavern, one of six local bars serving a total population of about forty-five hundred. We sat stunned for a second, all in the front row—Jill in the driver's seat, me on the passenger side, and Diane in the middle. I looked out to the road and could see car lights a ways ahead coming toward us. We all watched, thinking the car would swerve around the part of us still in the road, but as it got closer we knew.

"Oh my God, he's gonna hit us," said Jill. It's so weird, but in that moment we were all completely calm. I was keenly aware that being on the passenger side, I would get the direct impact, but we did nothing but stare at the headlights.

The next thing I remember, the police and medics were hovering over me along with Jill and Diane. The car was in the middle of the field and severely damaged. The police called our parents, who came to the scene and told us that the driver was drunk and that if the car had been two more inches in the road, I probably would have died. Luckily, I came out of it with only a slight concussion and some bruised ribs. My mom was relieved. After a consultation with the doctor, we drove home.

"Well, at least I don't have to worry about you being at the mall all night," she said.

But she'd had enough. Once I'd recovered from the concussion, we had a little chat. And by chat I mean that she put me on notice that she would be ruining my life.

"That's it! I have had it with this," she said.

"What are you talking about?"

"You have given your life to him: your time, your tears, and now your blood! As of now, this is over." My mom blamed Bon Jovi for the accident.

"What's over?" I asked, trying to keep from getting hysterical.

"No more Bon Jovi. You can listen to the music and watch the videos, but that's it."

"NO! You can't do this to me. I love him!"

"You think you're suffering? I've suffered over Jon Bon Jovi more than any mother should ever have to!"

I ran to my room, slammed the door shut, and cried and cried. *This is not over,* I thought, *even if I am livin' on a prayer.*

Bon Jovi pins galore

In 1987, the most popular Top 40 radio station in Cleveland—Power 108—was broadcasting out of Newbury, Ohio. Newbury is about thirty miles east of Cleveland, but it might as well have been a different world. Completely and proudly rural, we had two stoplights, no McDonald's, and a Dairy *King* instead of a Dairy Queen.

For me, having WPHR down the street was like having a link to the big city, a link to the music, a link to Jon. One night after getting off work from the local video store, I cajoled my friend Julie into driving to the station to meet the DJ on hand. We simply knocked on the heavy glass, and after a few moments a man who looked about thirty came to the door. He was a handsome bear of a guy with sandy blond hair.

"Hi!" I said. "We live up the street and think we'd like to pursue a career in broadcasting, so we wondered if you could show us how you do stuff." I was improvising.

"Sure, come on in," he said and turned around to walk back to the studio. Julie and I looked at each other, shrugging like we couldn't believe we got away with it. He opened the door to the studio, put his index finger to his mouth to quiet us, and pointed to two stools. We took our perches. He flipped the "On Air" sign, put on his earphones, and pressed some buttons.

A prerecorded voice said, "Today's Power Hits," which was followed up with a cougar "ROWR!" Then he spoke into the microphone: "Power 108 with Cat Thomas the Cat Man, playing twelve in a row with zero commercials guaranteed." Then he hit another button to play a song and turned to us.

"So, what do you girls want to know?"

Since he was the only one there, he let us listen in some more and showed us around the studio. He was nice, completely open, and seemed to genuinely like teenagers. Especially pretty female ones. With my new style and curves, I looked more womanly than many of my counterparts, and I noticed that he noticed. I didn't recognize it then, but that was probably my first turn as an opportunist. Cat, liking what he saw, sent signals to my brain that I could somehow use the attraction to get stuff.

"How old are you girls?" he asked.

"Eighteen!" I lied before Julie could answer. "We're seniors."

"Well, cool. I'm here every week night, so feel free to stop by or call," and then he handed us his card. We exited the station, locked arms, and giggled all the way home.

I worked part time at a video store, and about once every week, I'd stop by the station. Though I missed the first Bon Jovi stop in

Cleveland, I knew they were coming back around again, so I started planting seeds.

"Where do you think the best place would be to camp out for tickets?" I asked, trying to sound nonchalant.

"Why don't you come with me? We're sponsoring that concert and a contest."

"Oh, cool. I'll just have to ask my mom…She's kind of…"

"Well, I can get her tickets too. Tell her she can bring a friend."

"Really?"

"Yeah, sure—no sweat."

I pretended it was no big deal, but inside I was dying. Now all I had to do was convince Mom.

My mom had a pretty strong bullshit detector, so I decided to play it straight and tell her the truth. To my serious surprise and delight, she agreed, but under one condition: that she talk to Cat and he back up my story. I gave her his number, and after she got off the phone, she said, "OK, it's a go…" I jumped up and down for five minutes straight, thinking that was as good as it gets.

But it got better. Two weeks later, Cat called me at home. "Hey, Jen, listen, I can arrange for you to come in the limo with me and the contest winners. Your mom and her friend will have to meet us at the concert, but if you can go early, I'll pick you up, and then you can hang backstage with us and meet the band before going to your seats."

I couldn't speak.

"Hello?"

"Yeah, here. Me…good…with…that." *Why do I sound like a cavewoman?*

"OK, I'll give you more details as we get closer."

I hung up the phone and sat on one of the dining room chairs to catch my breath. It was March, and the concert was in two months. I had eight weeks to prepare.

Operation "Make Jon fall in love with me" included the following steps:

Lose seven pounds to get to 125
Find the perfect outfit
Identify all the different scenarios that could occur
Determine and practice a response to all scenarios identified

Step one would be easy: skip the cafeteria pizza and do some of my mom's Jane Fonda tapes. Step two required an inventory of my closet. Nothing outfit-wise struck me as just right, but I did have a white leather jacket that fit me perfectly and a pair of low, but sexy white pumps. I just needed a dress. A trip to the mall would fix that, and I found a light pink sleeveless number that went down to my knees and hugged my curves. Done.

For the last two steps, I would need to imagine all the possible ways Jon would act. For instance, if he was cocky, I imagined myself saying, "Think of all the fans who support you. You would be nothing

46

without us. NOTHING!" I couldn't really imagine him being anything but lovely, but one had to prepare. I practiced my responses in the mirror until I felt I was ready.

And then the day came.

I got dressed, teased my long, permed, and frosted hair to the sky, and stepped out to enter the limo as an eighties goddess. The contest winners were two female friends in their twenties who were as psyched as I was, and we were accompanied by Cat and another DJ, Rick Michaels. The mood was giddy as we jammed out to music on the thirty-minute ride to the Richfield Coliseum on a warm May day.

Several groupies were gathered around the area where the band buses and VIP guests pulled up. Suddenly, everyone in the limo took notice that from the waist up I looked exactly like Jon, especially with hair, leather jacket, and shades. Cat suggested that I pop out of the moon roof and give the groupies a show.

"You think it'll work?"

"Try it." The girls in the limo egged me on.

"OK..." I jumped up on the seat so that my top half was showing and raised my hand with my three middle fingers folded down and waved my pinky and thumb in the classic "Rock on!" sign. The groupies went crazy. When the limo parked and I got out—obviously no longer a *man,* they started shouting, "FUCK YOU!"

Heh, I thought. *I'm about to meet my soul mate, so fuck YOU!*

We made our way through the melee near backstage—sound guys and wires were crisscrossing us—until we arrived in a large holding room with about fifty other radio station representatives and various guests. I could hardly deal. My skin was crackling with excitement, and I sat with my hands underneath my thighs to keep from biting my nails.

We waited. For over an hour, we waited. I barely spoke to anyone because I was there for me, and I wanted to be inside my head preparing.

Cat, noticing my tension, said, "You know, I don't want you to be disappointed if it's just Tico who comes out." Now, I loved Bon Jovi for the sum of its parts, and one of those parts was the drummer, Tico Torres. But I had not come this far to *just* see TICO. No fucking way. As this thought bounced around my head, I became more anxious. But then I looked down the long hallway that led to the holding room, and there was Jon walking toward us. I grabbed my camera.

It sounds cliché, but it really felt like everyone disappeared, and it was just me and him, separated only by a hundred yards. No one had noticed him yet, and I watched him walk toward the room, as if in slow motion, dressed in tight leather pants and a cut-off shirt. He was smaller than I expected—maybe five-eight and thin—and he looked tired. I could feel tears well up, and I pinched myself on the thigh to get it together.

When he entered the room, several handlers marshaled him over to us. Apparently, as the concert sponsors, our group got first dibs. Cat and the others stood up, but I remained seated, frozen, and he stopped right at the base of my chair, shaking their hands, looking down at me, and smiling. He started to tell a funny story that I can no longer remember, and I sat there, mute. All that practice down the drain! Cat, noticing my catatonic state, decided he should step in.

"This is my friend Jen."

"Hey, Jen," he said, smiling warmly and extending his hand to the one that was holding the camera. Instead of simply moving the camera from one hand to the other, I dropped it and shook his out-stretched hand with my mouth wide open. I didn't even say hi. He looked at me with an expression that read *Am I crazy or does she look like me?* and then one of the handlers told us it was time for Jon to move to the other groups, but not before pictures were taken.

"Anyone want me to take a photo with their camera?" asked the female handler, and I momentarily regained my consciousness to hand her mine.

We stood up in a group—the concert winners to his right and me to his left—and I felt him put his arm around my shoulder. I man-aged to wrap my arm around his waist and willed my molecules to remember his shape so I could replay it later.

The handler took some photos with other peoples' cameras, and when she got to mine, she said "Honey, it's not working."

"Huh?"

"Your camera. It's not working."

"No, did, um, did you try…"

"Honey, I can't make it work, sorry," and then she gave it back and began to corral Jon to move to the next group. I looked at him, try-ing to think of something brilliant to say to make him stop and real-ize I was not just his female, mute doppelganger.

Who is who?

"Don't worry," he said over his shoulder as he walked away. "The station can get you a picture." And then he winked at me and walked on. I sat down on the chair again and watched the other groups as they showed off their gregariousness. Stupid talkers! Stupid me!

Cat patted me on the shoulder in a way that said, "Buck up, kid," and joined the other DJs. I slumped. When Jon made his way out, that was our cue to leave. Cat escorted me to the place I needed to go to get to my seat, and I turned to hug him. We stayed in touch for about a year, and even though I never got that photo, I'll always think fondly of him.

When I got to my seat, the opening band was playing—I can't remember if it was Cinderella or Tesla—and my mom and Margie were there. My mom's face lit up immediately and then toned down slightly when she saw my face.

"How was it?"

"It's over. I met him and he didn't fall in love me!" I howled.

"Oh, honey. Why don't you just…you know…try and enjoy the show?"

I sat in my seat, disgusted with myself, and cried and cried and cried. I didn't cry at school, but I cried at home. After a couple weeks, I had to move on.

In the early 2000s, some friends convinced me to go to a Bon Jovi concert for nostalgia's sake. I demurred at first, but they told me to get over myself and come with them. Just before the band came on at the sold out area, I wondered, *What am I doing here?* I still like him. He seems like he's a serious man. He does a lot for charity and is married with kids to his high school sweetheart. He's hardly ever in the tabloids and has been able to maintain popularity and relevance over the span of nearly thirty years. In fact, I admire him. But really, *What am I doing here?*

And then the lights went down, a guitar started playing, and he walked out on stage flashing a perfect smile on that beautiful mug.

And I was sixteen again.

COME TOGETHER, RIGHT NOW, OVER WEED

The summer between my sophomore and junior years of college, I worked at the Automated Teller Machine Processing Office at the bank where my dad was a vice president. This had absolutely zero to do with my major, but Dad persuaded me to take it to augment my business acumen even though we both knew I would be bored balancing debit and credit slips from the various branches. It did have one mark in the "pro" column, however…I got paid. The money that I made during the summers significantly funded my incidentals throughout the school year, so I looked at it as bird in hand. I was scheduled to start the job a week after I returned from school.

The night I got back, my boyfriend Leo and I hung out with some friends. Somebody lit a joint and passed it around. I only smoked rarely in college but thought, *What the hell? I just finished my second year. Why not?*

The next morning my dad called.

"Hey, honey, I forgot to mention that you have to take a drug test before you can start at the office. So you need to schedule that right away."

My heart stopped.

Try the political argument, I said to myself.

"Well that's just a violation of my rights!" I protested. "I mean, I am philosophically opposed to this kind of fascism! Forget it!"

"Drop it, hippie," my Dad said. "Just get it scheduled."

I steeled myself. "Um, Dad, um, yeah, there might be a problem."

"What kind of a problem?"

"Well, um, I kind of smoked last night."

My dad, knowing I smoked cigarettes (but not liking it), said, "That's OK, honey. Cigarette smoking doesn't show up on a drug test."

"Um, yeah, I know that."

Silence. Five seconds of silence.

"What the...?!? Jesus Christ, are you kidding me? What the hell is wrong with you?!?! Jesus...!!"

And then he hung up.

I called my mom in a panic and told her what happened. She snorted on the phone.

"It's not funny!" I squeaked, slightly hysterical.

"Oh, honey, please. Your dad and I used to smoke pot all the *time* in the seventies."

I began to relax.

"In fact," she continued, "I remember we were over at a friend's house and we got stoned, and your Dad stood in front of us and lip synched an entire Moody Blues album. It was *hilarious.* Seriously, he set up a stage with a spotlight and danced and everything."

I called my dad back. "You can't stay that mad at me because that would make you a hypocrite. I know about singing to the Moody Blues album."

"What are you talking about?

"Mom told me about that impromptu concert for your friends. Sounds like a fun party."

"JESUS CHRIST!" he yelled and hung up again.

My stepmother, Vicki, called me back that night. "Listen, honey, just drink a lot of cranberry juice, and let's hope this whole thing blows over."

I passed the test and started the job. A couple weeks later we had a party at my dad's house with cousins, aunts, uncles, and friends. My dad, who had *just* begun speaking to me without having to yell "Jesus Christ!" every five minutes, caught me alone and said, "By the way, it wasn't the Moody Blues, and it wasn't the whole album. It was the Beatles. *Come Together.* And that song seemed to last forever."

THE PATH OF MOST RESISTANCE

A University of Toledo (UT) student was arrested yesterday after assaulting a student on the path that connects the south side of the East Ramp to Westwood Avenue.

Tom Smith[1], a freshman in the College of Business Administration, was arrested for sexual imposition, after assaulting a UT student, according to a Lucas County Jail arrest report. According to the UT Police report, the victim said she was walking east on the path toward Westwood Avenue when she noticed that Smith was following her. She then started to walk up the embankment. Smith asked the victim to come with him, but she refused and he grabbed her.

The report states that the victim pulled away, but Smith grabbed her again, reached up her dress and grabbed her between the legs. The victim pulled away again and ran to her home, which was approximately five to 10 minutes away, and called UT Police at 4:15 p.m., the report said.

According to Joe Skonecki, assistant director of campus police, the dispatcher was able to get a detailed description of Smith and broadcast it to Rocket Patrol and the UT Police officers. According to the UT Police report, Yarko Kuk, Rocket Patrol supervisor, spotted Smith, notified UT Police and pointed Smith out to Jerry Owens, the arresting officer.

Owens confronted Smith at the sidewalk, which connects Lot 1-S to Lot 1-N near the Engineering-Science Building and told Smith that he resembled the description of a person who recently assaulted a student.

The three went to Smith's car because he was not carrying the described book bag or wearing sunglasses. According to Owens, the book bag and sunglasses were in the car. Smith agreed to go to the UT Police Station, the report said. UT officers then transported the victim from her house to the station and conducted a photo line-up, which consisted of a picture of Smith and pictures of six other men. Skonecki said the victim distinctively pointed Smith out.

---

1   Student Arrested, by Jacki Masar, Assistant News Editor. *The Collegian*, Volume 68, Issue 57. Perpetrator's name changed.

I woke up like normal: pressed the snooze alarm five times, made coffee, smoked a cigarette, and watched TV. I lived in a group home with five other women in a neighborhood that primarily housed college students. I loved those random early mornings when no one else was awake and I didn't have to talk with anyone. I put on a light green-and-white-striped knee-length cotton sundress, packed my schoolwork and books, and stepped off our front porch. I smiled at the early summer weather—bright, but still crisp due to the early hour.

It was an average school day for me. Three classes, lunch at the Student Union, and no tests. I remember feeling settled in those late months of my sophomore year. I had reined in the galloping charge of that first blush of independence and left frequent binge drinking and passive learning behind. After my last class, I headed home and passed the large east-parking garage on my right. Two campus police sat inside a security outpost twenty meters away, taking in the afternoon crowd.

I headed down the path adjacent to the garage while thinking my usual post-class thoughts: *I only have two days to finish that paper, I need to do laundry, don't eat three cheeseburgers for dinner... WAIT...Someone is behind me.*

It wasn't like it alarmed me. I heard the crunch of twigs that let me know someone was following down the path, but it was a path commonly followed. What focused me was the quickness of the follower's pace. My mom had worked for a rape crisis center, so my sister and I were schooled in the ways of predators and what to do if someone approached us. Following her advice, when I heard his pace quicken, I turned around as casually as possible to memorize his characteristics. He was tall and thin with reddish blond hair, wearing green and purple plaid shorts with a light T-shirt. He wore sunglasses and carried a backpack over his left shoulder. I turned back and tried to speed up my own pace without looking suspicious.

Woods surrounded us.

I was steps away from the embankment leading up to a road that was fifteen feet from a busy street. I started to claw my way up when I felt him reach up my dress and pull on my inner thigh. Somehow I maintained my position, but I was in danger of slipping. I looked toward the path and didn't see anyone coming. Another lesson from Mom popped in my head: if he doesn't have a weapon, fight. So I began to kick and scream. I wasn't scared yet. I was angry. With his free hand, he slammed my body into the smooth, shale parts of the embankment, which momentarily stunned me into passivity. And then he threw off his backpack. He centered himself and stuck his other hand up my skirt and jammed what felt like four fingers up my vagina through my underwear. He pressed his thumb on the bottom of my tailbone and started to pull me down. I fought the nausea and the panic and focused on survival. *No, no, no, no,* I thought. *Do not let him drag you into the woods, or he'll kill you.* I screamed louder. "Get the fuck off me!" I yelled, kicking harder until one foot landed on his balls and he stumbled backward, allowing me to climb to the street.

I froze for a moment, checking that I was actually free, and then ran fast, not looking back until I got to the 7-Eleven ten blocks down. Once I was confident he didn't follow me, I ran home, scared and full of adrenaline. It's remarkable how fear continues to propel you, even after the fight. *I just want to go to my room and get under the covers,* I thought.

I opened the door with force and looked around, wild. Three of my roommates were sitting in the living room, and I blew past them and ran up the stairs to my room. I immediately got under the covers, shoes and all, and pulled the duvet over my head. Not more than a minute later, my roommates ran upstairs and sat on my bed.

"Jen, what happened?" one of them asked.

"Someone attacked me," I said quietly. They pulled the covers back strongly and started speaking all at once.

"Oh my God, where?"

"Are you OK?"

"Someone bring me the phone. We're calling the police." They dialed the number, handed it to me, and then huddled in a protective bubble. I described exactly what happened to the officer, surprised by how calm my voice sounded, and then waited for them to pick me up and go to the station. My roommates came with me to keep me on track.

When we arrived, they ushered me into a conference room and asked me to retell the events to an officer, who filled out a report. It was all very clinical. After about an hour, someone came in with a series of photos to review. I picked out my attacker right away. The police told me how they had found him scoping out another victim but caught him before anything else happened. They also told me about two unsolved rape cases where the perpetrator matched my attacker's description and that they would be questioning him about his whereabouts on those days.

Back at the house, my roommates gathered around me. Girls are great for asking probing questions, so I talked. I am reminded by that day that talking is the first step to recovery. I wanted to crawl under the covers and will the attack into something tangible I could smash or burn or lock away; and I might have had they not been home. Talking made me process what happened. Talking let me know how many people loved me and supported me. There have been times I haven't talked immediately after a traumatic experience. In its wake lay missed opportunities and a lover or two who translated this as a fatal flaw. But after the attack, I told my boyfriend, more friends, and my family. I felt stronger every day, but I also wondered if I could have prevented it. Talking made me believe it wasn't my fault.

"Maybe I should have worn jeans…"

"No! It was hot."

"Why didn't I just take the sidewalk along the street?"

"You've taken that trail a million times. It's not your fault."

Regardless, we all agreed to never take that wooded path again.

Less than a week later, the student paper ran the following editorial:

"Women Responsible for Own Safety" by Jay Benoit, Student Columnist[2]

Editor's Note: This column reflects the opinions of the author, and is not intended to represent the views of *The Collegian* or its editorial staff.

Last week a female student was assaulted by a male student near the east parking ramp. While this incident was likely unavoidable, it points out the need for women to take a more active role in, and take responsibility for, their own well being.

First, if society is to believe that sex crimes are acts of violence—as they are—then remove the cloak of secrecy surrounding the victims. In news accounts of violent assaults, victims' names are listed even though they may fear retaliation from the perpetrator.

In the most recent incident, although it involved no more than an uninvited grope, the victim's name was veiled in secrecy, as if the act somehow merited more confidentiality than any other assault. In the minds of many people, this can only reinforce the image of sex crimes as "dirty little liaisons" between two adults, rather than a violent encroachment on a person's rights. Listing the victim omits the double standard and gives society a real person to associate with a real violent act.

Second, women must take action to ensure a safe environment for themselves and others. At a recent workshop offered by Crime Prevention Officer Sherry Patterson, there were less than 20 women in attendance. This is a sure sign of either laziness, complacency, or ignorance. These programs are not offered as a PR gesture on the part of the university— they are provided because there is the immediate danger of sexual assault any time a woman ventures into the dark surroundings of the campus. Since many parts of campus, like the east ramp, SWAC, and other areas are in remote, unpatrolled segments, these things can even happen in broad daylight.

Third, women must realize, especially on campus, that many assaults are committed by people known to them. Rape and other sex crimes are not always perpetrated by the stereotypical greasy stranger hiding in the bushes. When alcohol is involved, even sex with an intoxicated woman

---

2   June 3, 1991, The Collegian.

can be treated as rape. Men have a responsibility to police their own ranks, but group violence is a male domain, records show. Men are not often victimized by groups of drunken women. However, on campuses nationwide, there are incidents involving groups of men, particularly fraternity or athletic team members who assault women who are too drunk to resist.

Yet there is still a lazy attitude when it comes to appropriate dress and behavior at social functions and even in the classroom. Lulled into complacency and perhaps still thinking like "daddy's little girl," when all this was still "cute," young women come to class wearing skimpy tee-shirts and silky shorts.

This may be enticing, but not very wise in a largely itinerant community of strangers. Sex crimes are acts of violence, but on campus it is generally not the fat, old woman loading fish sandwiches into the vending machine that gets attacked, but the vulnerable coed whose posture and decorum indicate attack is possible.

Appropriate behavior, as with any crime, can avert an imminent attack or discourage the potential attacker. Acting defensively, knowing your attacker, and speaking out if attacked may help female UT students to be more safe both on campus as well as off.

———

I began reading this while walking across campus, and by the time I got to the third paragraph I had to sit down. *Uninvited grope?* I read the rest in a rage and marched to my creative writing class. My teacher cocked her eye at me as soon as I walked in the door.

"Is everything OK?"

I held the editorial up to her face and said, "This is me he's talking about. He's writing about me." Seeing I was all fury and indignation, she took me into her office and gave me a hug.

"I'm so sorry," she said. "I'm putting together a letter-writing campaign. This is outrageous." True to her word, the next edition came out with a greatly expanded *Letters to the Editor* section.

UT Collegian Editor's Note: The Collegian *received a great number of letters in response to the opinion column entitled, "Women Responsible for Own Safety," written by Jay Benoit, which appeared in the Monday, June 3 issue of* The Collegian. *Due to space considerations,* The Collegian *is unable to print all of the letters, and some letters, which appear below, have been edited.*

They were written by teachers and students and citizens who were simply too angry or disturbed to remain silent. They were defensive, educational, passionate, and personal. They were filled with empathy, outrage, and humor.

"Mr. Benoit, you wanted a name of a rape victim so you would be able to attach the actual crime to the actual name, so here it is[3]. Now that there is a desired name, please remember that every time a joke about rape is told, every time a rapist is excused and the victim blamed there is an insult on my character and my intelligence and to every other rape victim."

"No sexual assault, regardless of extensiveness, is acceptable Mr. Benoit, and women cannot be held responsible for such attacks."

"To the woman who was the victim of that sexual assault, please try to disregard such insensitive remarks. Like all of us, he has a lot to learn."

"Would Mr. Benoit care for an uninvited "knee," perhaps?"

They comforted me and buoyed my strength.

The rape charges didn't move forward. I was told that the victims were afraid to go forward for fear of retaliation or public outing. I understood that completely. So the charge against him was mine alone: gross sexual imposition, which is a felony. My attacker pleaded no contest

---

3   Author's note: name redacted.

in return for the lesser charge of sexual imposition, which is a misde-meanor. Much of this happened behind the scenes, with the police keeping me informed in a gentle, but authoritative way. Part of the plea bargain included expulsion, and that provided enough of a sense of security for me to push forward. He didn't know my name, and he'd been in my presence less than ten minutes. *All will be fine,* I thought.

Early one morning in January 1992, the partly clothed body of 19-year-old female UT nursing student Melissa Anne Herstrum was found at a remote site on UT's Scott Park Campus. She had been handcuffed and shot 14 times.

Campus police received a phone call just after midnight Jan. 27 from a cab company reporting a woman had called to inform them one of their vehicles in a parking lot on the Scott Park Campus was being robbed and that she heard shots fired about 15 seconds later.

Officers Jeffrey Hodge and Jeffrey Gasiorowski arrived near the scene, but did not see anything suspi-cious. After deciding to conduct a foot search of a wooded area near the Engineering Technology Laboratory Center, Gasiorowski found Melissa's body. Hodge wrote the initial report. They found Melissa's body face down in the snow, her pants pulled down, her shirt pulled up, cuts on her wrists,[4] and wounds from the 14 bullets fired into her back, legs and head.

Violence on campus solidifies a community and shines a spotlight on the victim. Every one of us could recognize our relatives, friends, or acquaintances in Melissa. We wanted to know her and go back and protect her. We wanted to reach out to her family and her sorority sisters and enlist as a vigilante army. We wanted to know why and how and who. We wanted to not be fearful.

---

4   Compilation of stories: "Family Sues UT, Hodge Over Murder," The Toledo Blade, January 19, 1994, Tom Troy, Staff Writer and "Herstrum's Life Casts Echoes...," Toledo Free Press, January 26, 2007, Justin R. Kalmes

It was the second quarter of my junior year, and I worked early mornings at the parking office on campus where students paid parking tickets and picked up permits. From 7:30 to 9:00 a.m., I worked the office alone. One morning just days after the murder and more than six months after my assault, my attacker entered the office. I was at the fax machine when he entered, and when I turned around to greet him, my throat closed up. I was grateful for the thick, tall wooden barricade with a flat-top surface that separated us and thankful that the door to get into my office space was locked. We looked at each other. *Please don't let him recognize me,* I thought, but I still didn't speak.

"I need to pick up a parking permit for the quarter," he said.

What the fuck? He's still a student?

"OK…" I moved slowly and meticulously so that I could always see him in my periphery. "It's sixty dollars…"

He wrote out a check. "I need a receipt."

I went behind another door where I could still see him but where he could not see my hand shake while writing. I came back around and passed him the items.

"Thanks," he said and walked out. Still shaking, I called the police and spoke to an officer who had been on my case from the beginning. He was gentle, suitably surprised, and told me he'd follow up immediately. When the full-time workers arrived at nine, I feigned sick and went home. I got a call from the officer the same day.

"I'm sorry to have to tell you this, but it's a case of red tape."

"What happened?"

"It's just a formality, but expulsions have to be signed off by the Student Judiciary Committee..."

"Mmm hmm..."

"The paperwork never got to them."

"And no one caught it? Until now?" I asked.

"Exactly."

"What do we do?"

"They told me you would have to meet with the dean of students directly. Can you do that and let me know it goes?"

"Yeah, OK, thanks...." Of course I stewed and ranted. But I also made an appointment with the dean for the following week. He welcomed me into his expansive office and engaged me in small talk for about five minutes before getting down to business.

"So, I'm sorry for what happened to you," he opened.

I thanked him. "What do we need to do to rectify the situation?"

"Well, what do you envision?"

Knowing why I came to see him, I was surprised there wasn't already a plan. "Expelling him," I said.

"Oh, well, it's a bit too late for that..."

"Why?"

"Well," he said, "we can't really go back and make it retroactive."

"Why?"

"Well, time has passed, and he is in counseling now and seems to be doing fine…"

I stared at him.

"He was having family problems at the time," he continued.

"Sir, with all due respect, a lot of people have family problems, but it doesn't make them go out and attack women."

"No, that's true, but again, he's in counseling now, and he's not allowed to live on campus, so it just seems like the best compromise…"

"You're not going to do anything?" I pressed.

"Well, it's just…"

"You have an unsolved murder on your campus and a known criminal who has assaulted women, and you're not going to do anything?"

"Again, I am so sorry for what happened to you, and we have numerous people working on the murder case, and you can always call me directly if you need anything." No matter what lever I pulled, he directed me back to his key messages: too late, counseling, sorry.

"I just hope no one else gets hurt. And if they do, I hope you can live with yourself knowing all these things." I walked out, feeling the momentary rush that comes with having the last word before going back to being stunned.

Melissa's murder was solved. Renowned forensic scientist Henry Lee—key witness in nearly every high-profile murder case from Nicole Brown Simpson/Ron Goldman to JonBenét Ramsey to Laci Peterson—happened to be teaching a seminar in Toledo that summer and worked with the investigators on the case. They hypothesized that the murderer was someone in law enforcement, and in early March 1992, one of the two first officers on the scene confessed. Hindsight being crystal clear, there were many signs he was acting out before he committed murder.

Through sheer luck or coincidence I never ran into my attacker again, but he was with me throughout the remainder of my college years. I looked for him in every classroom, every walk home, and behind each tree—the proverbial boogie man under my bed.

Melissa didn't have the chance to talk. But I did, I do, and I will.

YOU'RE NOT PRETTY ENOUGH

He walked into the college house party as if a spotlight shone on him at all times. People immediately turned toward him, their brightened faces reaching out to pat his shoulder, slap his hand, hug him, or talk to him. It's not like the partygoers weren't having fun before he arrived; it's more like the fun became…elevated—like being at a concert and digging the music but hoping and waiting for the band to play the song you *really* want to hear—the song that turns the amp up to eleven. When Leo walked into a place, he turned the amp up to eleven.

I was a freshman then, hanging out toward the back of the main room when he arrived. "Who is *that*?" I asked Natalie, a friend from high school who went to the same college.

"No idea."

I watched as Leo walked slowly through the crowd, taking in his olive skin; his dark, thick hair; his warm blue eyes; and his strong Roman nose. Now that I think about it, he resembled Ray Romano—and let me tell you, everybody loved "Raymond." He was average height, about five-ten and had a build that was perfectly suited to my evolving tastes: broad but not overly muscular. I was drawn to him. I saw him making his way toward the keg, so I grabbed Natalie's hand and headed in the same direction. I did my best to act nonchalant as I filled my plastic cup and nudged a mutual friend to introduce us.

"You guys don't look like country girls," Leo said with a broad smile, referring to the small, rural town in Ohio where we grew up.

"And what are country girls supposed to look like?" I asked in a tone that contained equal parts challenge and flirtation.

"Well, they're supposed to wear overalls and braids," he said, "and drive a pick-up truck with a bumper sticker on the back that says 'I'd rather be tipping cows.'"

"Sorry to disappoint you, but I've never tipped a cow in my life."

"What about you?" he asked Natalie.

"Oh yeah, sure," she said, proud.

Leo and I spent the rest of the party talking mostly to each other. People approached him frequently, and he'd introduce them to me and tell a funny story about how the two knew each other. Then he'd give them an unspoken signal—the one that says, *Good seeing you, but I just met this girl, I like her, and I'm doing my thing…*

At the end of the night, he walked me back to my dorm. He didn't try to kiss me. He just asked, "When can I see you again?" And when I replied, "Tomorrow?" he didn't flinch.

I turned to give him one last look before I closed the door behind me, and he was right there waiting and looking back with that same broad smile on his face. As we later recalled, in that moment we knew we were going to be a couple.

We were inseparable until he graduated a few months later and returned to Cleveland to find work in the private sector. We'd write each other at least once per week and talk on the phone every couple days.

"I'm in the library right now getting my job search organized. I'm surrounded by law students and so much law talk that I think I could pass the bar exam. I wish I could give you an answer if I'm coming up to Toledo, but unfortunately I can't, so as soon as I hear something I will correspond to you a response. See? I'm sounding like an attorney already."

"When are you coming home, honey? I'm going through withdrawals! Just remember that I miss you and I'm always thinking about you."

"Jen! Hi beautiful! How's it hangin' over there in Toledo? Oops! I forgot you're a girl and girls don't hang. I just want to tell you again how great it was to see you this past weekend and how much fun you are to be with! OH MY GOD! I just remembered! Thank you for the underwear you left in my pseudo suitcase. Lucky, I checked before I walked in the house, or Mom would have given birth to a calf when she did the laundry! Don't worry, Jen, they'll go good with my miniskirt and high heels. Tell Natalie I said hello! Miss you!"

"OK, down to business. Your mom wants to bond. This could be interesting. Sounds like a lot of fun. What am I saying? Every time I'm with you I have fun, why would this be any different? You just tell me what you want and we'll do it."

"I just want to thank you again for spending Easter with me and my family this past weekend. Everyone likes you a lot (but I love you Jen, don't forget that!). All I can say is you made history in my house! And I hope it continues! I just thought of something. Since I met you I haven't had a weekend that was not fun (except when we didn't get to see each other). Why the hell didn't I meet you sooner? I'm counting the minutes till we meet again."

"I love you! It was on my mind, so I just thought I'd say it. I realize we still see each other almost as much as before, but knowing that you're not minutes away sucks. But we'll still manage anyway, because I just love everything about you, and I hope that you'll have me around for a long, long, long time. OK, now that your beautiful head is really big,

I'll cut out the mushy stuff. By the way, it's really fun taking the time to write letters. I really enjoy this. See what you did to me? I never even wrote my parents let alone a girlfriend. You're a good influence. I am a little fish on a BIG HOOK in love with you. I really did get the BONUS plan when I met you, honey. You are truly the most beautiful person I have ever met (inside and out), and I hope that someday you will be my wife and we can share the rest of our lives together."

He gave me butterflies. And for most of those long-distance years, our relationship was really great. We traveled back and forth between his place in Cleveland and mine in Toledo on the weekends and took vacations together during winter, spring, and summer breaks. During the week when the university was in session, I could focus on school, part-time work, and my friends, and I was *fully* focused on those things because my love life was settled *and* my boyfriend wasn't up my grill every five seconds. I had clear, open highway in my head to engage elsewhere, which was such a gift.

Note to self: You are your happiest, romantically, when you are with someone who makes you feel wanted, secure, and supported, yet who also encourages and appreciates your independence (free to be you and me!).

Got it. Noted with a gold star.

Thanks.

The long distance helped keep the excitement alive: we had stuff to talk about, we had great sex, and we had fun. This comfort and happiness made me embrace everything, including food, and slowly but surely, I gained eighteen pounds. Then suddenly the fun stopped and so did the sex, and then letters and the closeness.

I confronted this weirdness, and at first he avoided the topic but then came clean. "I just think back to that party when we met. You were such a stunner." That hurt, but I refused to cry.

"Do you want to break up?" I asked.

"No...no, I really love you, it's just that...I want our children to look back at our wedding photos and see you looking beautiful..."

I was five-six and 127 pounds when I met Leo; with the added weight, I was up to 145 pounds. And while my boyfriend, who implied he would soon be my fiancé, made me feel like a fat piece of shit, I was also beginning to get a lot of attention. I became increasingly aware that for every male who wasn't quite into curves, there were others who had a different "type" in mind. And for those men, I was the gold standard.

So while I was confused, I desperately wanted to get back to the fun days, the sex days, the days when Leo would make me feel like I was the only person who mattered. Stupid fairy tales! Seriously, for as much as I loved *Star Wars,* I loved princesses roughly the same. The story of Princess Jen: Chubby Duckling into the Swan! I knew that if I applied myself I could do it, but I also knew in my core that I was not losing the weight for me, and it burned me up. However, as things got back to normal, much to everyone's relief, I placed that burning resentment in a box, buried it, and positioned a headstone on it: "Jen's Better Judgment, RIP."

*When I was "heavy," I preferred photos taken from the neck up –
including a set of Glamour Shots I gifted Leo with as an
effort to prove I was pretty. All I proved is that my hair is
fabulous and chokers aren't my thing.*

Leo proposed at the end of my senior year at Cleveland's most
fancy restaurant—the Top of the Town—and I said yes. After college I moved back to Newbury to live with my mom, plan the wedding, and find a job. Leo owned a small condo and was planning on
selling it to help fund the purchase of our new home. We set up appointments to look at houses for sale, and when we went to view-
ings, Leo's parents were always in tow. My mother-in-law, Sophia,
was a 110-pound spitfire. She and her husband, Luca, had emi-
grated separately to the US from Italy when they were both around

sixteen, and there was no way they were going to let their firstborn, American-influenced boy make such a large decision on his own.

After a couple of appointments, I pulled Leo aside. "Do your parents need to come with us to every open house?"

"Well, they know a lot about this stuff, so they thought it would be helpful." Luca built and managed several properties in the West Side Cleveland suburbs.

"Yeah, sure, once we decide to make an offer it makes sense for them to check it out, but on the first look?"

"Jen, it's fine. Don't worry about it. It will still be our decision."

And then, just six weeks before our wedding, shortly after all two hundred invitations had been mailed, Leo called me, excited, and said, "We just bought our new house, Kissy!" (Of all the pet names we could have chosen, "Kissy" was what we landed on). I was stunned.

"What do you mean?"

"Dad saw a place that was open right next to one of his properties, so it'll be perfect—I'll help with the upkeep there, and in exchange, they're going to help with the down payment."

"Did you sign the papers? I mean, is it a done deal?"

"Yep—I can't wait for you to see it!"

"Let me get this straight. You just bought the house that we are going to live in without me seeing it AND your parents are part owners?"

"Yeah….so?"

"So you don't you think I should have been part of that decision?"

"Look, it was too good to pass up, and we had to act fast. You're going to love it!"

"But what if we want to move and your parents don't want us to sell? What then?"

"Jen, my parents are not going to screw us, if that's what you're implying." I imagined steam coming out of my ears like in a Warner Brothers cartoon.

"I can't believe this. I can't believe you did this."

"I don't know why you're so pissed. After all, it was *my* money from *my* condo that helped make this happen."

"And your parents' money, don't forget that!" And then I hung up. People talk about red flags, and this one was raised high on the flag-pole, waving prominently. I was conflicted and thought about calling off the wedding. For two weeks I stewed and analyzed and fretted and sought advice. My parents maintained the dynamic that we es-tablished after I went to college: it's your decision, and we'll support you no matter what. My friends, like everyone else, were thoroughly charmed by Leo (or "Raymond"—remember, everybody loved him).

"So what? You have an awesome soon-to-be husband who bought you a HOUSE! What the hell's the problem?"

For me, it always came down to the embarrassment factor of call-ing off a wedding and losing the money already invested. Oddly, I didn't focus on the relationship at all. Three weeks before the big day, I still had no idea whether I was going to go through with it, though I kept that to myself. And always playing in my head was the fact that where I came from and in that time, marriage was the next step. We'd been dating for five years, and in Ohio in the early nineties, if you didn't break up by that time, you got married. Between 1993 and 1995 I was in at least ten weddings.

Two weeks before the wedding Leo took me to the house. The previous owners had just vacated, and he brought me there, blindfolded me, and set up candles and a picnic on the living room floor. He took off the blindfold and stood behind me with his hands on my shoulders.

"What do you think?" he asked, his face excited and hopeful, like a child presenting his first real attempt at an art project.

"I love it."

I hated it. The house itself was fine—nice, actually—but I didn't have a hand in it, and I would forever feel like a renter, a squatter. During that picnic Leo told me how he couldn't wait to start our life together and that this was just the beginning of how much fun we were going to have. Before long, we were having sex on the floor, and I was thinking about the moment Leo would see me walk toward him, soon to be his wife.

We got married in August of 1994 in a Catholic church with a full mass, complete with Holy Communion, even though half of my family is Jewish and the other half are lapsed Protestants. In other words, I was married in a ceremony in which I could not participate. I protested, but my mother-in-law was adamant, and if I pushed, she pushed harder. We had a really progressive priest, I justified to myself, so I lowered the new red flag down the flagpole and thought, *What's the big deal? It's the **occasion**, not the ceremony, right?*

I like big hair and I cannot lie.

At our rehearsal dinner my father-in-law yelled at me when he learned the salads would be served family style instead of individually. My inner voice said, *Go to your happy place,* and that carried me through to the wedding where we were joyful and excited about our future. We went on a cruise to the Caribbean, and I cried several times. I thought I was letting go of stress, but Leo told me I was acting like a baby. I was twenty-three. I felt like a baby.

The red flags I ignored before banded together and merged as huge, crimson swaths of fabric that covered the walls and the floors and were stacked high in the linen closet. Almost immediately after we got married, the dynamic shifted. Leo appeared to be becoming more…*traditional.*

For example, he wanted to have dinner every single Sunday at his parents'. Now, I liked his family, especially my sister-in-law, but I do *not* like having a lock on my calendar once a week. Never have. Rarely ever will. So I told him so.

"I mean, let's plan dinners, I like dinner! But every single week? Nuh uh." Not my jam.

Soon after we married, I got a job as a marketing manager for a small economic development agency, and my commute was longer than Leo's. One night I arrived home and found him sitting on the couch watching TV, waiting for me to walk in the door. He greeted me warmly.

"Hi, honey, what's for dinner?"

"I....don't...know....want to go out?"

"No, let's cook something."

"OK, what do you have in mind?"

"Whatever you feel like cooking."

I laughed. "Are you serious?"

He turned from the couch where he was watching TV and laughed back, but said, seriously, "Yeah, why?"

"Because we've been together for five years, and I have hardly ever cooked for you before. That's why."

"Yeah, well, we were just dating then. Now we're married."   And then he went back to watching TV.

My first thought was to hit him over the head with one of the heavy pans we received as a wedding gift, but then I panicked and thought, *Maybe this **is** my duty*, and I didn't want to be a bad wife, so at first I succumbed and attempted...cooking.

I was awful. And I don't like being awful at anything. Mediocre is barely acceptable, but awful? Out of the question. So I alternated between caustically serving tubs of SpaghettiOs_and then feeling guilty and actually attempting to make something that resembled a home-cooked meal, which yielded barely edible food and barely civil dinner conversations. I saw the disappointment in his eyes, so soon I gave up altogether. I didn't cook, I barely cleaned, and I sure as hell didn't put much thought into the house.

"Why don't you decorate or spruce up this place?" he'd shoot at me accusatorily.

"Why don't you?" I'd shoot back.

I'd drink and smoke in the house, and he'd chastise me, so I'd meet my friends out at bars and smoke and drink and complain. After only six months, a malaise settled into our sparsely decorated home: married life wasn't what we expected. We both felt it, but didn't speak it.

And then Charlotte entered our lives.

When I think about Charlotte, it becomes clear what was destined to happen. She was tall and thin and had long, bleached-blond hair. She looked like what I imagined Pamela Anderson would look like if Pamela Anderson were an accounting intern. She worked out, didn't smoke, and asked Leo for his opinion on decorating ideas she had for her new apartment.

The first time I met her was at a bar in early 1995. Leo was with his favorite people from the finance department at the hospital where he worked, and Charlotte, their intern, was the only woman invited besides me. Being twentysomethings, we were a fairly immature bunch, and once a few pitchers of beer were tossed back, the conversation predictably turned to sex.

"What's the weirdest sexual thing you've ever done?" one of the guys asked the six of us. A collective groan filled our space.

"I've got something," said Charlotte. "But I'm afraid it's too...I don't know, too much. And I don't want to tell you guys and then have you make fun of me or think I'm bad or something."

"Tell it to Jen first," Leo said. "She can be the judge."

So Charlotte proceeded to whisper in my ear a story about her and her former boyfriend fooling around in bed and their dog, who was also on the bed, started getting uncomfortably close, and she asked her boyfriend to move him. The boyfriend suggested that maybe the dog should be part of the mix, and at the end of the story the dog "sort of" went down on Charlotte.

I stared at her for a full five seconds, mouth agape. "Don't tell that story."

The men were staring at us, literally on the edge of their seats.

"Why?" she asked. "Too much? Scale of one to ten."

I whispered in her ear, "Honey, there's no scale for bestiality."

"Oh, please—they'll love it!" She retold the story and then went to the restroom. (After that, Charlotte bore the nickname "dog girl" among me and my friends.)

One of the guys said, "I would drink her bathwater."

My husband looked transformed, like he had experienced something so profound that he would never be able to go back again.

I tried to talk to my friends about the growing unhappiness in my marriage, but they generally—perhaps to be hopeful—blew it off as being a phase. The one sympathetic ear I had was in Cathryn, a beautiful, bohemian singer-songwriter who dated Leo's cousin. Having been through similar situations, she walked that perfect balance of encouraging me to trust my woman's intuition while holding out hope that it was "nothing."

One night in the summer of 1995 I called Leo at work to see if he wanted to meet at one of our local haunts to watch the Major League baseball playoffs.

"Oh man, I have a major deadline. When I'm done I'll call and see if you're still home, and then we can make a plan from there, OK?"

"Sure, sounds good."

I called Cathryn an hour later and asked her to meet me instead and left Leo a note telling him where we'd be.

When I walked into the bar to meet up with Cathryn, I saw Leo and Charlotte sitting across from each other in a booth, engaged in intense conversation. I felt a rush of emotions—surprise, hurt, anger—but I just kept advancing toward them as if on autopilot. Charlotte saw me out of her peripheral vision, mouthed the words "oh shit," and immediately pulled back and reached for her wallet. Leo appeared completely unfazed.

"Hey, what's up? I was just about to call you."

"Yeah, um, this is weird," I said.

"I was just about to call you," he said again. I looked at Charlotte, who looked back at me, and we all froze, wondering who would make the next move. Just then, Cathryn walked in.

"Hey, party people. I'm Cathryn," she said, all sunshine, as she extended her hand to Charlotte, who took it and introduced herself. Our waitress appeared.

"You again," she said to Cathryn and winked. "Like I need another drunk like you in here."

"You love me," Cathryn said. "Bring us another round." No one protested, so I slowly sat down next to Leo, who was watching the game.

"Whoa, did you see that play!" yelled Leo suddenly. "That was awesome!" One of the Cleveland Indians' best players had batted a monster hit that barely went foul.

"Jesus, I *hate* when Thome is up to bat," I said. "That guy grabs his crotch like he's milking a cow." Leo laughed and Charlotte shot him a look that said, *Why are you laughing at **her** jokes?*

Oh shit.

Leo said, "I can't believe how much Jen is into baseball this year. She used to hate sports." Then he looked at me. "Do you remember how much you used to nag me to turn off the game, get off the couch, and go out and do something?"

I laughed. "Well someone had to—you'd get couch sores."

Charlotte looked directly at me. "You used to get mad at him for watching sports? That's what men do! They watch sports!" Leo laughed again.

"I mean," she continued, "if he were *my* man, I'd let him watch all the sports he wanted."

"Have you dated anyone longer than a year?" I asked her.

"No."

"OK, well, let's swap stories when you have." Charlotte huffed and asked Cathryn to move so she could go to the restroom.

"What's your problem, Jen?" Leo asked.

"What's *my* problem?"

"She's not going to come out of the bathroom until you go apologize."

"Leo, what the fuck?"

"She's going through some stuff, and she's just a kid." She was twenty-two and I was twenty-five. "You're better than that."

I went. I still can't believe it, but I went. She was in the bathroom playing with her hair when I walked in. I guess I was curious.

"Are you OK?" I asked. She turned to me.

"Yeah, it's just..." And then she said something that was so devoid of any sarcasm or falseness that it arrested me. She said, "I just want you to like me." *Maybe Leo is right,* I reasoned. *Maybe she is just a 'kid' going through some things and Leo is a mentor of sorts.* Her manner was one that drew out the savior in people, I guess.

I touched Charlotte's arm. "I do like you." And we went back to the table with the air cleared. Charlotte, with renewed confidence, began talking to Leo, and Cathryn and I turned our attention to each other. After about fifteen minutes, Cathryn looked at me and mouthed unnoticed, "What's going on?" and nodded her head in their direction. It felt like we were encroaching on a date.

I mouthed back, "I don't know."

"This scene is LAME!" Cathryn said.

"I agree," I chimed in.

"Leo, let's go to the Irish place," she continued.

"I'm gonna stay here for a minute, but I'll meet you there in a few." Leo looked at me and smiled. "You guys go ahead...I'll be there." I did not want to leave him there alone, but I was afraid if I stayed I would be on a continuous cycle of trying to be cool, but upsetting Charlotte with increasingly malicious insults, and then having to chase her to the bathroom to boost her up, so I left.

"What the hell was that?" asked Cathryn as we left.

"Do you think I need to worry?"

"I don't know. Just keep your eye on that one."

Leo never met us. He arrived home at 3:00 a.m. and went directly to the guest bathroom to vomit. I found him there when I woke up, passed out on the floor, with his work clothes still on. I got ready for work quietly and left him there to clean up his own mess.

On my way home, I picked up groceries, intending to make the perfect meal because I somehow convinced myself that if I became a good cook that would solve our problems. When I walked through the door, Leo was there, un-showered, only wearing his boxers and a T-shirt. We didn't greet each other. Instead, he followed me around silently, sticking far enough away so that it couldn't be called hovering, but close enough to let me know that he wanted me to set the tone.

I ignored him and pulled out the groceries and began to cook dinner. As I was frying turkey cutlets—in an amateur fashion—I looked up at him and said, "Don't ever make me feel like I'm not your wife again."

He looked down and nodded.

But things only got worse.

He started going to the gym with a ferocity and dedication I'd never seen and claimed he'd finally decided to take control of his physical health and I should too, just not at the same gym. "That would be weird."

He stopped touching me. Again. The infrequent sex was not so much the issue for me, but his hand would move away when I'd grab it, and he wouldn't reciprocate when I'd wrap my arms around him in bed. So finally I stopped trying.

He came home late more frequently—sometimes really late—saying he had to work, but this was before cell phones, and I could never catch him at the office after five. He always had a plausible excuse. "I was in the bathroom," he'd say, "and I didn't check messages because I was in the zone trying to get everything done."

This, of course, caused fights. In which crazy shit is often said. Once I stayed up late waiting for him, and when he walked through the door, he sort of breathed heavy and said, "Oh, God Jen, I'm really in no mood."

"Why are you doing this? Why are you deliberately hurting me?" I tried to be plaintive but assertive. I didn't want to wallow in this anymore. I wanted to force this to its natural conclusion and get to whatever was on the next side.

"I don't know, Jen!" He ran his fingers through his hair, exasperated. "Sometimes I think you're just not pretty enough!" I let out a choke that can only be described as a guffaw mixed with one loud, short sob and watched as he walked toward the bedroom to go to sleep. The way he said it, the words he used: they pierced that vulnerable place in a woman's psyche. He wasn't saying I wasn't pretty. He was saying I wasn't pretty *enough.*

But then I thought, *Dude, you look like Ray Romano; you're no Tom Cruise!* (It was 1996, so it was Jerry Maguire Tom Cruise, OK?)

I remained on the couch in the darkness and buried my head in my knees and cried. *What am I supposed to do?* I didn't yet have the answers, but I did have the soundtrack. Alanis Morrisette's *Jagged Little Pill* was released during that time, and I wore her song "You Oughta Know" out, looping it over and over in the car and gripping the steering wheel tightly while I belted out the lyrics. It helped.

I'd meet my friends in bars more frequently to avoid being alone in the house obsessing. While there, I began to look for attention elsewhere, from other men, who could validate me with that flirty, alcohol-induced banter and, sometimes, a make-out session in a car. Sometimes a make-out session in an apartment. While that would boost me temporarily, it always left me feeling worse than before. And I never told anyone. I wasn't ready to confront what was happening. But my veneer—the face I put on when I stepped outside my house—was beginning to crack. It was beginning to affect my performance at work. I was drinking more.

Soon, I became a detective and snooped. I figured out Leo's voice mail passwords and checked regularly. I paid closer attention to his comings and goings to identify trends. This led to a lot of circumstantial evidence yet no "proof."

But he was getting sloppy.

In November of 1995, I was getting ready for a trip to London to visit a friend with my mom and sister. I was leaving in three days. While packing I got a call from Cathryn.

"Jim just called," she began. Jim was a waiter and in Cathryn's band—someone we all knew well. "Apparently Leo just left there with some girl. It was 'dog girl,' I know it!"

"What are you talking about?"

"Jim waited on them—I mean, they sat in his section and had this date! Jim was totally suspicious but thought maybe it was a work dinner or something until he asked them if they wanted dessert."

"And…?" I asked, impatient.

"Well, he asked if they wanted to see the dessert menus, and this girl kind of said, 'I don't know…so many calories, I don't want to have to work an extra thirty minutes at the gym,' and then Leo said…" Silence.

"Yeah?"

"Leo said, 'Don't worry, we'll just fuck it off later.'"

"…"

Cathryn continued, "They just left. Jen, it's time to get his ass in line!"

I began to talk, but it was that talk that comes off like you have something in your throat and you're trying to keep from crying but the effort burns. Still, I managed to squeak out, "I don't know how to handle this."

Cathryn said, "Tomorrow…we follow him."

And that sounded like a rational plan to me. The next day we plotted, calling each other several times at work to check and recheck our strategy. I called Leo and told him that we were invited to dinner with Cathryn and his cousin and that I would meet him at home at seven thirty so we could ride in one car. He said he'd have to work late too, so the timing was perfect.

I met up with Cathryn and drove in her car to the upper level of the hospital's back lot where we could sit on a perch and watch them exit the building. As we waited we chain-smoked and ran through the potential scenarios we might face and practiced our responses to each. We were ready.

We saw Charlotte and Leo exit the building together, get into their respective vehicles, and drive away. We followed them. After ten minutes, they both pulled into a bar parking lot that was a couple minutes from our home. Cathryn and I drove around a few minutes more to give them time to walk into the bar without spotting us.

Of all the scenarios Cathryn and I worked out, we missed one: being ignored completely. We walked toward them, sat one seat away from them, ordered beers loudly next to them, and then sat there, stumped. "This wasn't in the script," I said.

Finally Cathryn said loudly, "Jen, I don't know about you, but I'm kind of partial to German shepherds...!" Well, *that* caught their attention.

"Hi girls," Leo said, exasperated. "It's Charlotte's last day at the hospital, so I'm buying her a send-off drink." I willed my eyes to be laser beams and burn them both up. It happened to be the day of the Great American Smokeout, and Leo asked me sarcastically if I planned to quit smoking, while I was holding a lit cigarette.

I took a drag. "Yep, this is my last one," to which he replied, "You're a liar," to which I screamed, "NO, YOU'RE THE FUCKING LIAR!" Cue record screeching sound. Everyone turned to look at us.

Leo turned to Charlotte, rolled his eyes, and sighed. "I guess I have to go now..." and then paid for *their* drinks and walked toward the door. I looked at Cathryn, and she said, "Go...I'm going to stay and talk to 'dog girl.'" I scurried off my bar stool and ran after Leo and got into his truck where we immediately started screaming at each other and carried this ugliness into our house.

We walked into the bedroom where my luggage was laid out, a reminder I was leaving in two days for London. In a rage, Leo took off his wedding ring, threw it across the room, and screamed, "AS FAR AS I'M CONCERNED YOU CAN GO TO LONDON, FIND YOUR

HUGH GRANT, AND STAY THE FUCK THERE!" It's true, I did have a crush on Hugh Grant at the time (*Four Weddings and a Funeral, hellloooo*), but he had betrayed me too by getting a blowjob from Divine Brown a few months before.

Leo left right after that. Just…left. So I returned to packing. And crying. Later Cathryn called me. "I told her she was ruining a marriage," she said. "But 'dog girl' maintains that they're just friends."

Leo and I avoided each other until I left. I wrote him a long letter in which I presented an ultimatum: When I come home, you need to make a decision. Either you're in this marriage and you never see Charlotte again, or you're not and we separate.

When I arrived home, he gave me a hug. "Have you made a decision?" I asked into his neck. He gently broke the hug to look at me.

"Yes. I want to be with you."

I was surprised and suspected the turnaround had more to do with things souring between Leo and Charlotte versus a renewed commitment to our marriage. But I said, "OK," and we trudged along together into Christmas. Things did seem better. When I cooked, he ate my meals with a forced smile. He even put his arm around me or held my hand at our respective families' houses during the holidays. *Maybe Charlotte leaving for a new job will give us a clean slate,* I thought.

But he didn't want to talk about it. I'd try to bring it up and figure out how to repair the damage, but he didn't want to play. He didn't want to go to counseling and "go backward," he said, but I couldn't move forward. I decided even though I didn't have proof that he had cheated, he had still treated me like shit, and I deserved better, or at least the truth. It's crazy how obsessed I became with "learning the truth." I decided to give him a final opportunity to tell me, so one night after work I sat him down.

"Listen, I know this is not easy to talk about, but we have to...talk. I know you say that you and Charlotte were, are...just friends and that I'm just paranoid and we have our own issues, but I'm going tell you the 'story of us'...after we got married, like I'm telling it to a friend..."

"Do we really need to do this?"

"Let's just try. I want you to remember all of the things that led to this point, and I want you to tell me if you think I'm being irrational, and then I want you to fill in your side."

He didn't protest further, so I began. It was absolutely strange to relive the tale and to speak in the third person about my husband to my husband. He said nothing as I went through the chain of events and my feelings surrounding them. But I watched his face fall and his eyes redden. I could see that the stress of coordinating his two relationships and the lying and the covering up of all the lies was getting to him. I could tell that it hurt him to be painted in a less-than-flattering light, because people always responded so positively to him. I thought I could see that he was thinking about coming clean and was trying to identify the pros and cons on the spot, and I almost felt empathy for him. But this conversation was my last resort. If we were to move on, I needed *him* to tell me the truth about what happened and about how he felt. After I finished, he stayed silent.

"Well...?"

"Jen, I'm sorry."

I gave him some room, but no more came. "There's nothing else? Nothing you want to add?"

"No...I don't know what to say...just, I'm sorry."

That wasn't good enough, so soon after New Year's I arranged to move in with a friend for a little while, if only to gain some control back, and perspective. I called him from work one day and told him of my sadness and then of my plans. All he said was, "Wow, you don't know how to handle relationships at all," and hung up. I put my head down in my cubicle and closed my eyes. *I just want to know the truth,* I thought. *That's all I want, the fucking truth.*

I sat up straight and banged my fist on my desk. It occurred to me that there was one other person in this triangle who could give me what I wanted. I miraculously remembered the company that hired her, dialed information, got the main number, and called.

"May I speak to Charlotte Jones?"

"Hold please," said the receptionist, and I held my breath.

"This is Charlotte."

"Charlotte, it's Jen, Leo's wife. Listen, I need you to know that I am not mad at you at all; I just need to know the truth. Please, woman-to-woman, you're the only who can help me. Can we meet up?"

"No problem," she said. "How about tonight?"

"Yes! How about six?"

"That works. By the way, Leo is an asshole, and he doesn't deserve you."

"OK! See you later!" Then I replayed the last line she said. At that point I knew I would get the truth, and I was *giddy*. I went to Cathryn's first and drank a shot of whiskey. She made me promise to call her immediately after the conversation.

I arrived at the bar a few minutes early and ordered a beer. My stomach was churning. Charlotte walked in and approached me nervously. *She showed up!* I thought, and my inner child clapped. "Want to grab a booth?" I asked, trying to sound friendly and non-confrontational but coming off awkward.

The next two hours were a blur of confession from her side that revealed several nuggets, including him buying us the exact same Christmas presents.

"What the fuck?" I said, laughing. "Did he just go into all the stores and say, 'I'll take two of everything?'"

"I know, what an IDIOT!" she laughed back. It was like I was hanging with a friend. We also went through timelines. When I was in London, my dad and Leo had planned a trip to Canton, Ohio, to visit the Football Hall of Fame. Charlotte had spent the night with Leo, in our bed, and departed only thirty minutes before my dad was set to arrive. In that concentrated period of time, all of my hunches were validated, and I believed every word she said because not once did she make herself out to be the victim. Almost straight away she said, "I knew he was married, but I went for it."

Her saying that meant I didn't need to treat her as a hostile witness, and me proving that I was not mad at her afforded her the chance to let her guard down. She was in love with him, she confessed, but he lied constantly to her too, so she knew in her heart he was wrong for her. Like many unfaithful men before him, he had promised to leave me several times, and finally she stopped believing him.

After a bit, we had said everything that needed saying. We asked for the bill and started gathering our things together when she looked at me and said, "You know what would be hilarious?"

"What?"

"If we went to your house and confronted him together."

I considered this the best idea ever conceived. Without giving myself a chance to challenge it, I said, "Oh, we can make that happen." We practically ran out to my car and headed over to the house. We parked and went in through the front door, not knowing if he'd be home or not, but having a better chance to make a big entrance from that vantage point than from the garage. He was home, rumbling around in the kitchen.

We entered and I said, "Honey, you're never going to believe who I ran into." Then Charlotte and I made our way through the family room and turned right into the kitchen where he was at the refrigerator stuffing a leftover piece of chicken into his mouth. He saw us and froze.

"You motherfucker," I started, fully confident and ready to make him pay for all those months of making me feel crazy. "You told her you LOVED her, you asshole?!? You bought us both the same Christmas gifts?!? We don't even *like* kiwi body wash! Neither one of us, you dumbass!"

He looked at her. "Charlotte, I never told you I loved you."

She immediately retorted, "Really? I heard the 'love,' I heard the 'you,' and I heard the 'I.'" It was like we were a comedy team.

"Good one," I said.

He looked at me. "What do you want me to do?"

For a moment, I went internal. *That's it? No 'I'm sorry'? No begging for me to forgive him?* I almost broke down but then quickly pulled myself back into the present. "I want you to pack a bag and get the fuck out of here."

"OK." He promptly went off to the bedroom. One of my cats came around the corner and rubbed against Charlotte's leg.

"Hi, Callie," said Charlotte and reached down to pet her.

My face dropped. "Of course you know my cat's name...You've stayed here." Charlotte started to cry.

Because *I* had just pulled myself together, I expected her to do the same. I got real close and said, "Charlotte, I know this is hard, but you need to get it together." I pointed toward the bedroom. "His wife and his girlfriend are in his house confronting him...TOGETHER. This is a MOMENT, DAMMIT!"

She stood at attention and sucked in her tears. He had to go through us to get to the garage and his truck. We stared him down as he made his exit, and then it was over. In less than ten minutes, the confrontation was over, and we were left feeling like deflating balloons.

I turned to her. "I guess I'll take you back." We giggled nervously until we got to her car. "Wow, that really happened," I said.

"Yeah, whose idea was *that*?" And then we hugged, naturally and spontaneously, and she exited the vehicle.

When I got home, I called Cathryn. "The eagle has landed."

"On my way."

And thank God, because the calls started flooding in from Leo's mother, Sophia, who tried different defense arguments to get her son—who had obviously called her—back into my good graces. I put her on speaker so Cathryn could listen in.

"Jennifer," she said in her heavy Italian accent, "if I found out that Leo's father did this, I would laugh for tree days. Do you hear me, TREE DAYS!"

"Why?"

"Because who's a gonna cook for him? Who's a gonna clean? Definitely not some girl he play a kissy face with…and after tree days…he come back."

"OK, thanks, I'm going to go now."

But she kept calling. Her final defense was that boys will be boys and we just have to forgive them. This enraged me, so I yelled into the phone, "Sophia, they FUCKED IN OUR BED! HOW DO YOU FORGIVE THAT?"

"Oh, Jennifer, oh, don't say, oh…language!"

I hung up the phone, and it rang again immediately. It was Leo. I picked up so that only I could hear him.

"What do you want?"

"Jen, we need to talk. You don't know the whole story."

"Fuck you. You've had plenty of chances to talk."

"Jen," he said, "you don't know what you're doing. You're too immature. I'm coming home so we can work this out and you don't make the wrong decision." And then he hung up.

I looked at Cathryn and said, "He's on his way over. Let's get the hell out of here!" We scrambled around quickly, me grabbing the first shoes I could find, my purse, and some clothes to sleep in. Her car was parked in the lot of the shopping center next to our house, and we ran toward it as fast as we could. I was wearing a bright blue sweater, a black skirt, and black stockings. She turned to look back at me and make sure I was keeping up, went directly to the white pumps that rounded out my ensemble, and said, "You look like Minnie Mouse!" I slept on her couch and lay awake the entire night, replaying past events in my head like a movie.

The next morning I went back to the house, opened the garage door, and saw that his truck wasn't there. *Phew, he's gone.* I opened the door wearily to enter the house, and as soon as I did, he came bounding around the corner looking like he hadn't slept much either.

I dropped my stuff and tried to move past him quickly, but he grabbed me and mashed me into a possessive hug. I struggled to get out, but he moved me to the couch and threw me down so that I was half sitting and half lying. He then burrowed his face into my chest and sobbed. My stomach lurched.

"Please don't go! PLEASE. PLEASE. I love you. I'm so sorry. I'll never do this to you again, please."

I started sobbing too. "You're NOT sorry! You're only sorry you got caught. LET ME GO!"

"Never! I will never let you go—you're my wife!" And then he kissed me. He kissed me like I imagined you kiss someone who you thought you didn't want but now did. It had been so long since we kissed like that, I volleyed back with the same intensity and lost control of everything. Including my bowels.

I literally shit my pants.

I pushed him off of me and ran to the bathroom and locked the door, horrified. He ran after me and pounded on it. "Let me in!!"

"Leave me alone!"

I took off my clothes and immediately got in the shower to wash off the filth and then wrapped my hair and myself in some towels. I waited a beat and then unlocked the door only to sense him shuffling on the other side, so I relocked it. We waited it out—him on the floor in the hallway and me in the bathroom, both of us too exhausted to conduct a conversation through the door. I fell asleep, and finally, he left the house. I had cried a lot up until that day, but after that I wouldn't cry again for five years.

I temporarily moved to a friend's. Leo tried to woo me back, but his attempts felt half-assed. Still, there was a part of me that just could not walk away without thinking about that moment on the couch, without thinking about the fact that everything was finally out in the open, and wondering if maybe something could be salvaged. It's hard letting go of your first love, especially when you're legally tied to him. So after nearly a month away, I returned. And nearly a month after returning, I knew my marriage was over. It became clear that his avoidance of the topic was chronic. And it became clear that I needed to talk about it constantly to ever move on from it. We were in limbo. So again, I turned to the only person I felt could help me process.

I called Charlotte—who had cut off all communication with Leo—and asked her to tell me again the things he said to her and the things they did together so that I could remember and tap into that hurt. We handled these conversations completely unemotionally, and she took my calls all the time or returned them when I left messages. She was the only person—outside of myself—who allowed me to explore the affair and work through the impact it had on me. I finished each call with Charlotte feeling better. I don't think I ever asked her once how she was doing.

I had come to several conclusions. Both of us contributed to the downfall in communication; he wasn't alone in that. Before all was revealed, Leo had gotten himself into a pickle. I understood that once he was there, there was no easy way to tell me. Here I was *needing* the truth and thinking that the real crime—besides the affair—was withholding it from me. But I hadn't put myself in his place. Would *I* have been able to tell the truth if the shoe were on the other foot? I honestly can't answer that, but I'd like to think I wouldn't let my spouse flail and struggle. I'd like to think I would have been less passive than Leo, who was waiting for a path to present itself, rather than choosing one. During the times when he was more engaged in Charlotte, he'd hurt me and pushed our boundaries. I believe he did this in the hopes that I'd become fed up and leave. Then he could just continue on with Charlotte, introducing her to his family and friends as someone he just started seeing at the appropriate time. When he thought about what was at stake, including losing his relationship with my family and some friends and tarnishing his reputation, I believe he gave Charlotte the cold shoulder, hoping she'd break it off with him so he could resign himself to a life of mildly satisfying mediocrity (breaking that up with short-term future dalliances, only this time much more discrete). It's OK to discover your marriage isn't what you wanted, I concluded. But it was not OK for me to stay married to someone who was afraid to take the reins in his own life.

With a decision made, a weight was lifted, and I was able to find a new place to live and schedule a move-out date. I still feared Leo would be able to talk me out of going somehow, so I packed and planned the moving day for when he would be attending a week-long conference in California. Some friends helped, and I had a moment where I froze—*holy shit, what I am I doing?!*—and my friend Cathy had to slap me like Cher did Nicholas Cage in *Moonstruck*.

"Snap out of it!"

I picked him up at the airport the night after I moved out, my last wifely duty, and peppered him with questions to keep him talking. We pulled into the garage and then opened the door and entered the house. Leo looked around and turned to me.

"Where's the coffee table?" he asked.

For me, this transition was fairly easy, but for Leo the finality triggered his grief. After I moved out for good, he often called me and cried, or sent me letters, or parked outside the house I shared with a new roommate. But it was too late. Men generally mourn relationships after they break apart, but women mourn relationships while we're still in them.

Four years later I randomly ran into Charlotte on a Cleveland street. "Hi!" I called out enthusiastically.

"Oh my God…Hi!" She looked a little different, with shorter, less blond hair, and older.

"How are you? What have you been up to?"

"Let's see…I got married a couple years ago to a guy who I *thought* was the love of my life…"

"Yeah?"

"Yeah, he…uh, well, he cheated on me."

"No shit!?!"

"Yep…" she said. "I guess what goes around comes around."

I smiled. "I guess so." We wrapped up with some small talk, hugged, and then went our separate ways.

As far as I know, neither one of us ever looked back.

BE CAREFUL WHAT YOU WISH FOR

So let's take a moment and recap: I was raised by some pretty cool, loving parents who validated and supported me and encouraged my independence. This produced many wonderful things, like The Sex Papers. And moxie. Which led to me meeting Jon Bon Jovi. Even the weird stuff, like some of the experiences with my stepfather or violence on campus, built character. They are what made or reinforced that side of my personality that is all pluck and courage and *I will be heard.*

But at twenty-six, I was reeling. I just didn't know it at the time.

I was recently divorced. My ex-husband Leo and I had both contributed to the downfall of our marriage, but then he had an affair. Throughout our seven-year tenure, we weren't very good at communicating *about* the relationship. In the early years, when we were happy, talking about our relationship seemed irrelevant unless it was to express our glee. When we were unhappy—soon after we married—that lack of communication foretold our unraveling.

Throughout the divorce process and for months after, I'd blow off the topic if friends or family asked how I was feeling. I thought I was doing myself a favor by not dwelling on it, by "moving on." And I thought I was doing them a favor by not burdening them with the sadness of another marriage gone wrong.

"Great!" I'd say. "Couldn't be better," and that's usually all I had to convey to nudge the questioner to the next topic. But the truth was I could have been better.

I was angry.

Angry over the death of a future vision, which included being a hap-
pily married mom at an early age so I'd have the energy—and a
partner—to manage both career and personal life. Sure, I was still
young and had opportunities to meet people, but after my divorce
I wouldn't easily commit myself to someone else. I didn't see the
point.

Angry with Leo, who was so cavalier and never wanted to discuss
anything difficult. My mom provided some consolation: "You know,
Leo might not ever experience the real lows in life," she said, "but
he also won't experience the real highs." As a last-ditch effort to try
and save our marriage, Leo had arranged a trip to Las Vegas where
upon entry we were lulled into a *no time for talk; too many lights
and noises and cocktails to drink* trance. Unless me sniping, "You
fucked another woman!" at him every five minutes and him reply-
ing, "Come on, we're here for fun—let's go hit the slots," qualified
as talk.

And I was angry with myself for ignoring the red flags and marrying
someone I knew in that little place in the back of my mind where I
locked away the "bad feelings" that he was not right for me. That he
could do me in. I left him when I could see that staying in the marriage would diminish the fight in me.

The day we left the courtroom—divorce papers in hand—he said,
"Let's go have breakfast." I went. I didn't have anything else to do.

"Do you think you'll ever get married again?" he asked.

"Wow, I haven't even thought about it. What about you?"

"Oh yeah, definitely," he said, but not in an unkind way. He just stated it matter-of-factly.

I carried this anger into a new job at a marketing firm, which I started the very same week I got divorced. The firm was made up primarily of married men in their thirties and forties and comely women in their twenties. We worked long hours. We drank as a group together at least three times per week—sometimes at lunch, sometimes after work, and sometimes from lunch until way after work.

A typical working lunch.

I didn't know it then, but this dynamic was like a siren song calling for me to channel my frenzied ire.

Within a few months of starting, I was promoted to account manager and my boss, Jake, put me on many of his key accounts. He gave me full access to clients and sometimes took me to expensive, long lunches to drink-talk through ideas. Many times Jake would take long liquid lunches with the other executives or potential clients, and he'd call me late in the afternoon to meet him at a bar so he could regale me with antics and victories from his day until he needed to head home.

"Great work, sir!" I'd say with a smirk. "You put in another solid day!"

"OK, you asshole," he'd beam. "Don't stay out too late. I need those concepts by noon tomorrow."

"You didn't tell me that!" would often be my reply.

"Well…I'm telling you now," would often be his.

When these "deadlines" emerged, I needed to work directly with Ray, who ran one of the divisions. He was in his early forties and handsome in a suburban dad kind of way. He had dark, thick hair and olive skin. He wore khakis or jeans with polo shirts and was fit but carried an extra fifteen to twenty pounds that said to the world *I'm OK with drinking a few beers and skipping the workout.* He was funny, talented, and emotional, but dark and inappropriate as well. He was also married with children.

"Ray, we've got one of those 'make it happen specials' you love. We have to meet now."

"By when?"

"Jake wants them by noon."

"What the…? How are we supposed to get that done?"

"Like we always do—by pulling it out of our ass. I'll get the flip chart, you grab the coffee."

"Geez, you're bossy this morning."

I was. I learned it was the only way to get the job done; plus, Ray practically glowed with a desire to be bossed.

"You're leading this meeting, right?"

"Yes," I said.

"Thank God."

I quickly began charting out concepts and explained my ideas along the way. Ray nodded along in excitement and began adding elements that improved the themes. I began to put the presentation together on my laptop while Ray sat next to me and rested his head in his hands, gazing at me with sleepy fascination until my irritation forced me to say, "What? What are you looking at?"

"Just the most compelling woman I've met in a long time."

"Wow. Where's your number-one husband mug?"

"You're mean."

"Ray, you're married."

"I know, but I'm not happy."

"That's not my problem."

"I'm happy when I'm with you."

"You're just infatuated. Keep it to yourself." And really, when this kind of chatter first started, I wanted it to stop. But it also felt validating after spending seven years with someone who told me late in our marriage that I wasn't pretty enough for him.

"But see, just that right there," he said. "The way you act, like you don't care—that just makes me want to know you more."

Oh God, he thinks I'm mysterious. I am many things. Mysterious is not one of them.

"Really? Well, that makes you stupid. Obviously, I'm going to have to be the workhorse behind these concepts...*AGAIN!*" And then I grabbed the ever-present blue plastic grocery bag that comported various work papers and snacks and headed toward my office. The bag split open, as one did every week or so, and I bent down in a huff to gather my things.

"Time for another 'briefcase' already?" asked Ray, using air quotes.

"Funny," I said, because it was.

The longer we worked and drank together, the more we melded into a dominant/ submissive magnet, and it became harder for me to delude myself that nothing was happening between us, even if it was hard to define. At first the connection was just an outlet for me to be acerbic, with Ray standing in as a surrogate for Leo. But every so often, I'd let my guard down and open up and let him comfort me. And then I'd listen to him talk about his life and be able to respond in an authentic and warm way. These rare occasions usually occurred after drinking with our coworkers. We would sit in his car or mine in a nearly empty parking lot, listen to the radio, and stare out the window at the sparse lights that make up the Cleveland skyline. No one knew about us. Not that it would have mattered to our coworkers. That office reeked of hedonism.

We kissed a handful of times. The first time I felt obligated somehow. He was giving me what I thought I wanted—a place to project my feelings for my ex-husband. Wasn't it fair that I gave him something he wanted in return? Plus, he looked at me with such yearning.

"You're pathetic," I said, but I was smiling.

"Come on, don't say that."

"You are. You're convinced I'm this 'angel' who has come into your life…"

"Well, not *an* angel, *my* angel."

"That's what I mean! That's so ridiculous. You're married. You don't even know me. I treat you like shit…"

"No you don't; you're just hurting. Let me heal you…"

And the truth was I did want healing. I just stared at him, and then he leaned in slow, eyes open, and kissed me. But it didn't feel good.

After about six months of this push and pull, our relationship reached its breaking point, at least for me. The more he wanted to spend time together, the more I wanted to bolt, which then made him more desperate (isn't that always the way?). Daily, he'd e-mail or call and plead for a hug or a walk around the block so he could touch my hand or my hair. Sometimes I'd say no and he'd back off. Sometimes Ray would plant himself in my office and feign depression or some sort of "block" and say he'd need to see me at our "place" right away if he was to get on with his day. That place was the parking garage attached to our building.

"Fine," I'd say, rolling my eyes. Then he'd leave first, with me following minutes behind. I would meet him on the third floor stairwell, and he'd immediately latch on to me, his hands like spiders crawling to my ass where he'd knead desperately until I could feel him get hard and then I'd push him away, disgusted.

"Better now?" I'd ask as he stood panting against the wall before I turned on my heel to leave, counting down the hours until I could have enough drinks to dull my recall. I realized this state of affairs was becoming untenable.

Untenable, as it turns out, was also the firm's financial condition, though the executives were slow to acknowledge it. They spent wildly on entertainment and never slowed down when company revenue started dropping. As a means to reduce costs, "The List" was produced. On it were the names of several positions that needed to be cut, with a rotating list of names attached. A vice president who was close with the middle management and junior staff leaked "The List" daily to a select few, but never by e-mail. Depending on your favor, you rotated on and off "The List," and because the office included fewer than forty people, word got around. People were freaked out because one day you were on "The List" without any understanding as to why, and the next you were off without having done anything special. It was draconian, as was this sentence that one of the firm's executives laid in a memo after returning from a five-hour drinking binge:

"Not to come off as draconian, but we will no longer tolerate staff going out and drinking at lunch."

Ray and I were discussing this memo at our own liquid lunch the next day when "The List" came up. I told him I was going back to the office to confront my boss Jake, a real charmer with a gift for persuasion.

"Go for it," he said.

Fueled by three beers, I marched into Jake's office, sat down, and closed the door.

"I need to talk to you."

"OK…"

"I know about 'The List.'" Jake's eyes widened, a bit, and he sat up a little straighter.

"Who told you?" he asked.

"It doesn't matter."

"Yes, it does. Who told you?"

"I'm not going to say, and it doesn't matter."

This went on for what felt like several minutes. With neither party looking like we would back down, I split-screened my brain to grab a grouping of words that would pull us out of the rabbit hole.

"Jake, I was here late one night and went into your office to find something, and I saw it on your desk." Jake stayed still for a few seconds. *Bingo!*

"I'm sorry you saw that."

"Me too, and it's making us all crazy. So either pull the trigger or figure out an alternative, because we can't keep walking on egg-shells." And then I walked out. The next morning Jake pulled me into his office.

"Jen, I've done a lot of thinking about our conversation. I didn't sleep at all last night." I stared at him with my arms crossed over my chest. "I just want you to know that you're permanently off the list."

"That just means that someone else takes my place, so..."

"Jesus, does nothing make you happy? Well, I hope you take it as some form of consolation."

Word got around about what I had done. A week later, Jake gathered everyone into the conference room for a rare all-staff meeting. "I've been doing a lot of thinking," he began. "The truth is, we are a team, and I care about all of you and the work you do. And though we're not in the best financial place right now, I am going to make some changes that will hopefully turn that around. I'll let you know what those are in the coming weeks, but no one will lose their job. We sink or swim together." Many people looked at me and winked or came by later to say, "Nice work with Jake."

I was proud, and there were not many moments associated with that office that were making me proud lately. (Besides the actual work. *That* I was quite good at when I wasn't distracted.) Jake's pledge was slow to take, and after a little over a year, I visualized working for a company that had a more rigid structure and smart, dedicated people who would help me grow—people who would teach me things and mentor me over coffee or a salad or a wrap versus a Jack and Coke.

I found another job within two months (these were the Clinton years after all). I gave my notice at the end of the day on a Friday, e-mailed

Ray to let him know, and went home relieved. On Monday, a card was waiting for me from Ray. It read:

"You know, about a year ago, I was just not feeling well. I couldn't put my finger on it, but something wasn't right. So I went to my doctor and he prescribed a new drug that was not yet approved by the FDA, called Jen™. He told me it was very powerful, so I didn't take it right away—I just admired it for a long time. Finally, a few months ago, I tried it, and I learned very quickly that it is definitely a mind-altering drug. It raises sensory perception to new levels. Since the FDA has not yet approved it, I have been taking it in private—under the table, so to speak—several times a week. I don't know many other people on it, but I want to be on Jen all day every day. It sharpens my senses to the extreme. Let's say I am looking into the beautiful dark eyes of someone I care about a great deal. I feel like I was struck by a thunderbolt. And if this person holds my hand, it's like she has one of those gag joy buzzers in her palm—it's shocking. And if I dare grab this person and pull her tight to me and bury my face in her thick, dark hair and put my lips on her neck—well, there's probably enough electricity running through me to light up Youngstown. And if I kiss her, well, it's hard to describe because it's different every time. The first time I kissed her, my body felt like it was riding on all the rides at Cedar Point simultaneously. Not the lame-o rides like the Pirate Ship and the Mine Ride, but all the good ones, especially Demon Drop. Jen is a dangerous narcotic indeed, and I hope it never falls into the wrong hands. Fortunately and unfortunately, I am addicted. I take it orally now, but I'd even take it in suppository form if it came to that. I just need it all the time. It unquestionably makes me more sexually aroused every time I just look at the bottle, which is great, but one drawback is that Jen can be frustrating. But Jen is so good that when it's working I don't mind the frustration. Bad news, though. Now that I am hooked, my prescription is about to run out, and I don't know when I'm going to get more. I know I won't be able to get my hands on any for quite a while, which is painful. If I have to quit cold turkey and go through withdrawal, they will have to put me in a strait jacket in a rubber room, shave my head bald, and draw a big "J" on my forehead in black magic marker as a warning to others who may be tempted to try this drug. The doctors will walk by the room with the new interns, maybe tap on the window to make me look up, and sadly shake their heads. One intern may ask, 'What's up with this one?' The doctor will reply, 'Jen. He'll never be the same, poor sap.' The interns cower and avoid my room as if the doctor had said 'Black Plague.' I slowly lower my head and add to the puddle of drool on my lap...

"I think that in the farthest deepest wrinkles of everyone's brain we all develop our own concept of the consummate member of the opposite sex. Most people wait a futile lifetime for that person to come along. Very few people ever meet their ideal person; most settle for someone else who may grow to become that ideal. We never stop looking, though. Like everyone else, I used to have a model of perfection, someone I'd never find. But I did. As you know, I am ecstatic that I found my ideal woman. But silly me! I had the bar set too low. Jen, everything about you has gone beyond my expectations. I don't want to ramble on…You know how I feel about you. You're not the perfect woman, you are my perfect woman. Please don't forget about me—I will never forget you. I got a silly card so I could write something to express my gratitude and tell you how I feel. But I could fill one thousand cards and still come up short. I've missed too many opportunities *with women in my life, so the last few months have been the greatest. I'll miss the daily stuff—just seeing you, the random rendezvous, especially the confiding in each other. But this is not the end of the journey; it's only the beginning. Oh yeah, I almost forgot. Good luck in your new job. I know it will work out great because you're like, good 'n' shit."*

I felt sad. Ray had never expressed himself to me this way before. To the non-marketing mind, the prescription analogy may come off as crazy, but when you're a copywriter you often want to go bigger. It's hard to do that with corporate clients, so people with that sensibility tend toward the dramatic in their personal correspondence. Still, I was sad because it highlighted how differently we perceived the affair. For me, it was a transitory port in a storm. For him, it was obviously something more indeed.

We had a couple beers on my last day, but it was awkward. How do you say good-bye to someone with whom you were barely, but strangely, physical yet bared your present emotional state so freely? Who *took* it. You steer conversation to the funny, and hug him on your way out is what you do. A month after I left the job, I received a card from Ray. On the cover was a woman looking over her shoulder with the words "Where on earth has she been?" It read:

"One would think that with all the thousands of specialized greeting cards on the market today I could find one that says exactly what I want to express. Something about how I've been thinking about you, how I miss you, miss holding you, miss being close to you, and how I especially miss your spirit, for lack of a better word—something along those lines. I guess I'll keep looking and let you know if I find one, Jenny. At least the chick on the cover of the card looks exactly like you (if you hold the card at arm's length and squint)."

Ray e-mailed me from time to time, and when I had news I'd tell him, including the fact that I had started to date someone named Josh. The day I told him that, he took it in stride and said he was planning to attend a going-away party for our mutual friend Rachel from the firm. The next day, Rachel called to give me the details.

"…plus, Ray was groping me all night."

"What? Ray?"

"Yeah, he kept saying he wanted to leave with me."

I felt at least a half dozen emotions. Duped. Pissed. Jealous. Surprised, from thinking those last three things. Hurt. Ashamed. I sent Ray a vague e-mail saying so on a Thursday evening. On Friday he was frantic, so I agreed to meet him the following Monday for lunch and finished out the week confused. Over the weekend I gorged myself on TV and a diet that consisted entirely of crackers, cheese, and ice cream. I also practiced the conversation I would have with Ray in my head.

OK, here's what I'm thinking. You be Ray.

OK, go.

Ray, I'm sorry, but this…relationship…we have…doesn't mean the same thing to me as it does to you.

Good, direct. State your thesis upfront.

…so, I need to start on a path that is more healthy…

What if he says he'll leave his wife?

I don't WANT him to leave his wife.

I'm just saying, it could happen…You've led him on; in fact, you've kind of been an asshole. And you know, as Alanis would say, "Isn't it ironic…"

…OK! I'll take that under advisement! But nothing in that song is ironic.

That's not the point…

*Jesus help me—I **am** my own worst critic. What I really want to get across is: In a weird way, you were the friend who helped me most. You asked question upon question, to get to know me, and when I raged you took all the hits, often without a shield. I hate that part of my personality—the part that would use you like that—but I can't give you what you want. Nothing more will ever happen between us. Not just because I'm not interested but also because the consequences of continuing…whatever this is…are too grave.*

Yeah, go with that.

At lunch it came off a little more curt. "It's unhealthy," I started. He nodded in agreement as I continued, but I saw him shut down. We spent the rest of lunch filling in the awkward space—gossiping about the firm, talking about our weekends—and I returned to my office relieved. Until I received this e-mail:

Dearest Most Holy Bitch Queen:

Some lunch, Fucker! Next time I'll just tie a computer monitor to my ankle and jump off the Main Avenue Bridge! How dare you fuck with my emotions like that, Bitch? You fucked with me and NOBODY fucks with me!!!! I thought we had something great and you go and shit on me like I don't even matter…

like I don't exist! Go ahead, slut, toss me aside and move on to the next one. Men mean nothing to chicks like you. You used me like Kleenex then moved on. Oh! Oh! Jenny! Here I am! Please scrape the dog shit off your high heels on my face, please! Oh, thank you, goddess! Wench! Am I supposed to disappear whenever you say? Poof, and I'm gone? Who the fuck are you, David Copperfield? I must warn this Josh fellow that you are a sneaky minx before it's too late and you fuck up another good man. I hope he's real good at imitations and can do an imitation of a man about to get his heart ripped out and stomped on by a slut with spiked heels. There's probably a trail of men in your wake, all fucked up and emasculated, imitating Forrest Gump, unable to raise a decent erection because of your little whore games. I, however, saw through the games and have an endless supply of fine erections, thank you. Go suck on your blue bag briefcase, Bitch! If you think I'm serious, you're wrong. I'm not. Just joking to see if you still had your sense of humor. Ha Ha. Jenny, I once told you that I would never do anything to hurt you. I meant it then, and I mean it now. I love our relationship, and I love being close buds. At one point in our relationship, you told me you loved me, as a friend. I take that sort of thing to heart and hope we can continue as confidants and grow a private, personal closeness. And drink beer too! I know you are a proponent of recycling, and if ever things don't work out with whomever, I am 100 percent recyclable. I love you."

I stopped responding to his e-mails and calls (he stopped finally too), but it made me realize two things for sure:

1. I am making bad choices, and I want to stop.
2. Please don't let me meet someone I could fall for now. I am *not* ready.

HOW TO BE AN ASSHOLE

Those sharp, jagged emotions I hoped would lay dormant after my divorce? I guess they rose to the surface. I guess they wanted to be processed, but I didn't know how to do that yet, so I just kept pushing them to the side. *Time to focus on work,* I thought. *I'll deal with…that…later.* It's like I vomited but never cleaned it up.

I was creating a lot of messes.

Starting with the aforementioned Josh. We worked together and drank together (old habits die hard), and man, he was sweet, but sweet only gets you so far in a relationship that's rife with incompatibility. I was and still am very independent. I *need* to be alone as much as I *like* being with people, and Josh was an I-want-to-be-around-you-24/7 kind of guy. There's nothing wrong with that if that's your thing, but it's like nails on a chalkboard to me, so with that dynamic in play, what started as something sweet soon rolled into something sour. Add to the mix that most of our conversations revolved around *the relationship* and well, this girl can get cranky. If I went out with friends, I'd come back to questions:

"Three hours seems like a long time to hang out with people you see a lot, don't you think?"

"No."

"I mean, and I don't want to upset you, it's just—don't you think everything that needs saying can be said in three hours?"

"What?!"

"I just want to spend time with you, that's all."

"WE DO. I was with you last night and the night before and today at fucking lunch! Jesus!"

"Please don't be mad."

I felt trapped. Yet I still stayed in it because I didn't want to hurt his feelings. How many ridiculous situations did I put myself through because I didn't want to hurt someone's feelings or because I was avoiding a tough discussion? Or because I thought that opting *not* to be with someone = being alone for the rest of my life?

When I needed a new place to live—quickly—Josh suggested I move in with him and another friend of ours, Kristin, who was lovely and worked with us as well. I said yes and signed a year lease for a move-in date two months later.

About a week after that, I attended a mandatory conference in Washington, DC for all new consultants at the firm where I now worked. It was highly professional but also included playtime. The conference was Sunday through Friday and taught us about how to work with clients and in teams based on our Myers-Briggs scores. At night, we had "homework" but were also allowed to pal around with the three hundred or so other consultants in attendance from around the country. I meshed well with a guy from Boston who was a couple years older, Michael. He was Ivy League educated, a former pro-athlete, and really, really good-looking—someone I considered waaaay out of my league—and he spoke the language of that phase in my life: sarcasm. After the conference, we stayed in touch.

HIM, 7/27, 4:10 p.m.
Hey, you saw a great baseball game back in Cleveland on Friday night, huh? I hope you stayed to the end...!

ME, 7/27, 4:24 p.m.
I never made it to the game (plane was delayed), but I did meet up with friends. Nothing tops off a week of drinking like a weekend of drinking. I'm pretty sure my efforts to destroy my liver were far healthier than your sissy hiking adventure. How was it?

HIM, 7/27, 5:21 p.m.
My "sissy hiking adventure" is next weekend. PAY ATTENTION, JERK! I merely made mention of it because a) you are a dullard, and as such it is especially difficult to carry on a conversation with you, and b) a trip of such magnitude requires significant orchestration, so I must plan well in advance.

Do you hike? You mentioned you like the woods (er, and the ocean?), but I couldn't tell if you were a true nature lover or if you were just humoring me.

ME, 7/27, 5:40 p.m.
I am a nature lover. Like one time I watched a special on the Galapagos Islands on the Discovery Channel. I also like granola. Yep, they call me "nature girl" around here. Is this thing on? (Simulation of trying to tell jokes to a silent crowd and tapping the microphone, just in case you're a "dullard." And, by the way, please quit using words that make you appear smarter than me. Thank you.)

Seriously, though, I love outdoor activities, but don't necessarily seek out adventures that keep me away from electricity for more than three days. I went to Aspen last October, so I spent a lot of time hiking there. Climbed up mountains and gazed at the Continental Divide. The mountains made me cry. I'm not joking, jerk, so quit yer laughin'. During the summer I spend a lot of time on the water, and as I mentioned, I have a long love affair with the ocean. Always enhances whatever I'm feeling at the moment. Now don't go thinkin' I'm some sort of sissy girl. I'm tough, I tell ya—tough as nails!

Re: your hiking trip NEXT WEEKEND, if someone asks you a yes/no question and you answer with "does a bear shit in the woods?" there actually may be a bear shitting in the woods.

HIM, 7/28, 9:37 a.m.
Actually any yes/no questions will be answered with "do *I* shit in the woods?" So you're a nature girl? Crying on mountaintops? What a friggin' baby. Actually, I see you as a slightly older, more robust Laura Ingalls, running down the grassy hillside to particularly poignant music, the wind gently tossing your pigtails, one hand holding a daisy and the other a lit cigarette. Let me know how the presentation went.

ME, 7/28, 10:53 a.m.
You're pretty much on target with your description of me.

HIM, 8/1, 9:13 a.m.
Some immediate thoughts on our correspondence: First, you're very funny. Much funnier than you appear to be in person; in fact, I almost wish I never met you—that way I wouldn't have to meld this image I have of you as a chain-smoking lunatic with the lovely, bright, witty person that is depicted on my monitor each day...

Here's a question for you...On a scale of one to five, with one being "Strongly Disagree" and five being "Strongly Agree," how would you respond to the following statement:

I have a boyfriend.

So that thing starts to happen, right? That thing where you realize you're starting to go down the wrong path? I could *see* that I was starting to like this guy and was looking forward to connecting with him, often multiple times per day. I could *see* that I was starting to play with the truth. Yet I justified continuing because *we're just e-mailing, right? It's not like there are any expectations here, right?*

ME, 8/1, 1:52 p.m.

I would have to choose two, meaning Disagree. I am *seeing* someone but would not place it in that boyfriend/girlfriend thing. It's more of a "I'm feeling buzzed, do you want to make out?" sort of thing. Though he is a very nice, fun boy. And you?

HIM, 8/1, 2:03 p.m.

Now I'm feeling as happy as a little girl...I don't know where that expression came from—is that a Sprockets thing? What am I missing? As for me, I too am a very nice, fun boy. And I'm a one. And I've been feeling very buzzed (of course, the liter of Dewars hidden in my desk has helped somewhat). Hmmm...

Now is what I like to call "work time."

It went on like this: Michael and me e-mailing, then talking on the phone, and then making plans to see each other—though, in the beginning I was noncommittal because all the while, I was thinking to myself, *YOU ARE MOVING IN WITH JOSH AND KRISTIN IN A MONTH. WHAT THE HELL DO YOU THINK YOU'RE DOING?*

Well, self replied, *you're creating an untenable situation that will blow up in your face.*

That's right! Thanks for the clarification.

HIM, 9/5, 10:27 a.m.

Have you decided on Boston? I'm trying to think of what a first-timer would like to see...There's Beacon Hill (cool, hilly residential area where Cheers is), the North End (Italian food, mafia), the Freedom Train stuff (Old North

Church, Bunker Hill Monument, etc.), Harvard Square (Hippies—you'd like that), Fenway Park (beer, dogs, ball). We could also go to the Cape (read: the Ocean), or better we could fly to Nantucket or to the White Mountains in NH. That is, if you're still coming.

ME, 9/5, 10:46 a.m.
The Ocean is a definite. Does it make you nervous? I'm really nervous.

HIM, 9/5, 12:23 p.m.
Let's go to Nantucket; you'd love it there. It would be nice to get on some neutral ground, so to speak. I am a little nervous but mostly because I'm not confident you're committed to coming. Whatever. If you dis me, I'm going anyway. I could use the towels.

ME, 9/5, 5:37 p.m.
I booked the flight. See you in two weeks.

I wasn't *completely* delusional. I knew I'd have to explain my leaving town to Josh at some point, so I just ripped off the bandage and told him the truth one night. Sort of.

"Listen, I'm going to visit someone I met at the consulting conference. That guy I told you about. We've become friends."

"Hmmm, I'm not sure I like that."

"Yeah, well..."

"Where are you staying?"

"In a hotel." Which, you know, I *was,* just in Nantucket...with someone else.

It's a testament to the strength of the mind how easy it is to rational-ize your actions even when you know they're wrong. Even though Josh and I were no longer physical—something he accepted—I kept him on a long leash, as a "backup" in case things didn't work out with Michael. I wish I'd had the strength to sever any romantic notions compassionately but firmly. I wish I'd had the strength to say, "I'm not moving in" and just deal with the consequences, to not be afraid of "the unknown." Instead I was a coward and convinced myself that because I was being "honest" I was being fair. But just because you're transparent about treating people poorly doesn't mean you're not an asshole for doing it.

Boston was magical. Michael picked me up at the airport, and we went back to his apartment, cracked open a bottle of wine, and fell into a dreamy spell of conversation and making out. The next morning we headed off to Cape and took the ferry to Nantucket where we had great meals and great conversations. We rented mopeds and traveled around the island, marveling at the expansive homes with their dis-tressed gray shingles and pristine landscaping. The tone in our vir-tual correspondence transitioned effortlessly in person, and this left us both feeling open, relaxed, and excited. We shared many tender moments, including a long, lovely kiss on the shore of the ocean.

But it was not perfect. He showed signs of relationship sabotage by pointing out that long distance affairs were hard and might not be worth it in the long run (while we were in each other's presence for the first time—the first time!). And while he took care of me in the bedroom, he would not let me reciprocate. Instead I kissed his face and neck for ten minutes straight. He said, "Can you please do that forever?" I wanted to.

As luck would have it, he got a project in Cleveland and I got one in Boston, and because work paid for a hotel, I'd stay with him and vice versa. It felt like a mini getaway, a fantasy even in my own city, and I'd just lie to Josh about where I'd be and drum up reasons to avoid bringing Michael over to my place to meet my roommates.

"Ahh, that place is always a mess. Plus, remember how I told you Josh gets weird when I'm around other guys?"

"Oh…OK…"

We decided that in order to take our relationship to the "next level" I should move to Boston. We talked about where we'd live, what jobs we'd have, and how much we missed each other and wanted our lives together to start NOW.

This will blow up in your face soon.

[Me putting a pillow over my conscience's face] *Shhhhhhhh. Don't fight it.*

As is usually the case, things have a way of catching up with you. Michael was growing impatient with me and my inability (or unwillingness?) to make progress on our plans.

"Have you called [so and so]?" he'd ask.

"Uh…on my list to do today…."

"You said that yesterday. And the day before."

"Today. I promise, today." I did want all the same things, sincerely. I just wasn't ready to move to Boston *for a guy.* He was the only person I knew there (I hadn't met any of his friends yet either, come to think of it). It felt scary and risky to put all my eggs in that basket. After the divorce, my mind shifted into a logic machine: *what if, what if, what if?* There were too many what-ifs.

And of course the living situation with Josh was not ideal.

"Why are you letting this 'friendship' with Josh impede our relationship?" Michael asked one night.

"I'm not. I'm just trying to be sensitive to his feelings. It's hard when one person has a crush and the object of the crush doesn't feel the same way."

God, you're an asshole.

Shhhhhh.

"You're not doing anyone any favors. You're part of the problem, you know."

"I know."

In late November we took a getaway to an island in the middle of Lake Erie called Put N' Bay. I told Josh I was going to hang out with a friend who lived there (which I did, but I didn't see her). We connected deeper, on a level that made me feel like I had found "the one." I decided it was time to come clean and move out. Turns out The Universe felt the same way.

We had three hours from the time we arrived back in Cleveland on Sunday until Michael had to catch his flight. On the drive back from the island, I tried to think of things we could do to kill time.

"Want to go to the Rock Hall?" I asked.

"You know, I hate to keep bringing this up, but it's odd that I haven't been to your place yet," he said. "My friends think it's kind of absurd, actually. We've spent plenty of time at mine, and I don't like having to imagine what your sleeping situation is like."

"Well, how about we just drive by?"

"Fine...we'll drive by, weirdo."

And so we did. And as we're approaching, I saw Josh coming to the curb to take out the trash. We locked eyes, and all my options flashed before me.

Should I duck?

No, no, no. That's wrong.

OK, so...? Running out of time here!

Pull in.

"Well, there's Josh" I said to Michael.

"Great, it will be good to meet him actually."

[Begin slow motion reel]

We both get out of the car and Josh is looking at me like *what the fuck?* and Michael approaches Josh and warmly extends his hand, and Josh takes it and says, "What have you two been up to?" and Michael says "Well, we were just in Put n' Bay and had the best time," and Josh says, "Oh, that's cool," and we all head into the house, and Michael goes to use the bathroom, and Josh says to me, "Wow…you're a real asshole," and I say, "I know, and I'm going to take him to the airport right now," and then Michael comes out of the bathroom and sits on the couch and starts talking to Josh about the football game that's on TV.

After a couple minutes of listening to their small talk, I said, "Let's go to lunch!" a little too loudly, a little too abruptly. I just wanted *out of there.*

Michael looked at me weird and then smacked his hands to his knees before rising. "OK, I guess we're leaving. It was nice to meet you."

Never once did Josh "give me up." That freaked me out! If the situation had been reversed, I would have confronted that shit *immediately.* But not Josh; he kept up appearances and later asked me if it was OK if he was mad.

"Is it OK? Honey, I thought my shit would be on the lawn. Yes, it's OK. But we can't pretend anymore." I moved out a month later. My friend Cathryn rented me the bottom half of a duplex in Old Brooklyn, which was just up the road from The Memphis Tavern (aka *The Drew Carey Show* bar). I offered Josh and Kristin my share of the monthly rent for bagging on the place after only a month, and they took me up on it. So, double rent for ten months, but conscience clear.

What was not clear was my future with Michael. On the ride to the airport that day, it was clear I was freaked, and that made him question my integrity. Further, he felt I had waited too long to move out, and in doing so I lessened his confidence in the relationship. In mid-December I flew into Boston for a project, and when he met me at my hotel I could tell he was perceptibly cooler toward me. In a panic, I climbed on top of him at 3:00 a.m. and rubbed against him until he was hard. I grabbed a condom and guided him inside me. Though he didn't protest, he was not an active participant. He lay there, with his eyes closed and his arms by his side as I circled my hips slowly and then faster and made noises that I hoped sounded sexy. Neither one of us was satisfied with the experience. I flew back to Cleveland knowing it was over.

Back at my own apartment, I sank into a funk for a few weeks. The only thing worse than a general funk is a funk that you yourself created. And because I was (in retrospect) embarrassed about the way I behaved, I didn't talk to anyone about it; I just internalized it.

Hey, you need an activity.

So I started taking cardio kickboxing classes, which helped, but I remained in a funk.

Why don't you spruce your place up?

So I waited for inspiration to find me, and it did in the form of a *Real World* marathon and some mushrooms a friend gave me. I painted my walls bright blue and green but did not get the hues right. A friend came over and asked whether my place used to be an ice cream parlor.

"No, I painted it!" I said proudly.

"Are you on Prozac?"

"No!" *But maybe I should be?* I thought that if I could only see him one more time I could convince him I was ready to pursue it. And *that* would end my funk.

If he just looks me in the eyes, he'll know.

In the beginning of December, I returned to Boston one more time for a project and let him know I'd be in town from Wednesday through Saturday. He was at a conference in DC, returning on Friday, and to my surprise he agreed to meet me that night. I was elated. *This is your last chance,* I thought. *Don't screw it up.*

A day later a snowstorm hit the Northeast and planes were delayed across the region. He called to tell me he didn't know when he'd get back, but it wouldn't be for a couple days at least. I hung up the phone, gathered my knees to my chest, and rocked myself back and forth for an hour straight, calming only when I came across *How Stella Got Her Groove Back* on cable. At least where Stella was it was sunny.

ME, 12/30, 9:30 a.m.
I miss you. It's been eating at me for the last week. I really want to see you, but I feel nervous, bad, what have you. I thought about sending you a Christmas present, but they were plum out of *The Big Lebowski: The Director's Cut*. Actually, I kind of tortured myself with whether or not to send you one. But I didn't want you to feel guilty or weird, and I wanted it to be the perfect gift that said exactly what I wanted it to say without actually saying it, so I took the low road and got nothing. Lately, I've just been reliving moments and thinking about you. A lot. I just miss you.

Got to go now; have a conference call with Mike and Cassandra in your office, actually. They're helping me with some project stuff, and I've been slacking. Give the girl a promotion and a raise and she quits working...

HIM, 12/30, 10:14 a.m.
Well, you must not be doing the call, because I just saw Cassandra sitting at her desk.

I wouldn't worry about the gift (I know you're not really, anyway). I didn't get you anything either, though I thought about it, but I figured I'd have the chance to do that later if/when we saw each other.

I don't really know what I'm feeling, and, of course, the holidays are always a screwy time for that sort of thinking, so I try not to put too much stock into how I'm feeling either way now. Things are different, more realistic. You're more settled, and that's good. I don't want to force things just because they were better between us before—that's not right. The distance thing is hard for me—I'm sure for both of us—it makes it hard to make a strong, tangible commitment. But I like that we're (beginning to) talk normally again and write normally, etc.

I think that's best for now.

HOW *NOT* TO BE AN ASSHOLE

If there's one thing I've learned, it's this: if someone wants to be with you, they will do whatever it takes to be with you. They won't follow some Nicholas Sparks-type plot, meandering through a series of obstacles (*We're from totally different worlds; it will never work!*) until they finally "see the light" (*All I need is your love! I get it now!*) And then the two of you go off and live your dream life, the end.

No, if someone doesn't want to be in a relationship with you, they'll send clear signals; you may just not want to recognize them. At least that's how I was. I'd send Michael letters and call him and e-mail him, all in the spirit of "Hey, I've got some funny story to tell you" but with an agenda of "I will wear you down until you like me again." He'd always respond, was always gracious, and at first I mistook his simply being kind to me as hope. But there was no hope. He was gone and wasn't ever coming back.

For a while I thought if I could just prove how good I was, how on track I was to being that person we both saw potential in, then dammit, we might just have something here. I devised schemes (that I neither implemented nor shared with anyone, thank goodness) where—as one example—I would send him a postcard with a date, time, and place somewhere in Boston in the future, and then I'd just show up on said date and time and wait for him.

If he doesn't show, then I'll know!

You already know, dumbass!

I almost bought a love potion that was guaranteed to win him back for $69.95, but that was a lot of money for me back then, and it was also…crazy. I said some cruel things to myself during that time (though publicly I tried to project a persona that was put together and happy).

You are such a fuck-up!

Why doesn't he love me back? How can it just GO AWAY?

WHY does it just go away?

You made it go away you dumb, fat bitch.

This time in my life is what finally forced me to confront my grief about the downfall of my marriage and the changes it brought. For a while, I thought Michael was the main factor behind my sadness, and the fact that I was "fat" was the main reason he was gone. That he was *the one who got away,* and by my own design no less. I thought that I blew my one chance at happiness post-divorce, and because of that I deserved to live a life alone, a life of being single, a life of hellish existence. How awful!

How dramatic.

Because, hindsight being what it is, he wasn't my "soul mate." He wasn't *the one who got away.* He was the one who made me realize I wanted to fall in love again—my breakthrough guy, if you will—and if I wanted it, I'd have to be an active participant in getting it. Awareness. Good.

But there was also this: I didn't/don't believe in a "soul mate" as in singular. If we all had just one soul mate, then with my luck mine would have been some kid who lived in Siberia and died at age ten, two hundred years ago. "Soul mate" as singular is a term trumped up for fantasy or convenience. Want to express your love to someone? "You're my soul mate." Looking for someone to love? "God, I just want to find my soul mate! Is that too much to ask?!" *He died. Siberia. Two hundred years ago.*

Soul mates as plural, however—meaning there are several people you could potentially partner up with out there in the world—that's something I can get behind. And I don't mean *just* with romantic partners; friends can be soul mates too, but let's focus on romantic relationships. We are all multifaceted, yes? We all have different primary sides to us—the stuff that makes us who we are. If I had to narrow mine down to eight, they would probably be these:

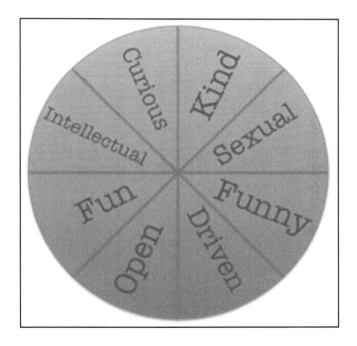

I want someone who brings out these sides of me, who encourages them. And these descriptions reveal not only my primary traits but also many of the traits I seek in a long-term partner. Think about the traits you seek. Then think about whether you've been with someone who is all of those things, all within the same package. (There's someone out there who said yes? ALL of them? Really? Well, congratulations! You should play the lottery every week).

The point is I came to that sort of philosophical arrangement in my head when it came time to approach dating as a twenty-eight-year-old divorcee who was ashamed of her status and didn't have the best track record. It helped me manage my expectations. *I don't need my boyfriend to be my everything,* I reasoned. I have friends and family and peers to help fill those voids, as well my own solo pursuits (like going to movies by myself sometimes, or reading or walking with my iPod). This is where I landed. But it wasn't such a direct route from almost buying love potions I hoped would trick someone into loving me to...a better place. Getting from A to B? That's the mucky stuff, which had to be dealt with, but I didn't recognize it as a necessary step at first.

I didn't recognize, frankly, how closed off I was. Even with my own family. A few years ago, my mom and I were touring Arlington National Cemetery and took a challenging walk through the grounds. It was one of those oppressively humid days. The sweat was gathering on my inner thighs and under my breasts, chafing me. I could see the waves of heat and feel the heaviness of it weighing down my limbs, my hair, my lungs. But that's not what nagged at me most. What nagged at me most was the affection my mom threw my way. She held my hand as we passed by thousands of grayish-white graves. She linked her arm in mine as we approached the Eternal Flame. She put her arm around my waist as we stood at the Tomb of the Unknown Soldier.

And all it did was make me feel really uncomfortable.

I recalled a conversation my Mom and I had not long before. "You know I do *not* want to get remarried," she said, "but I do...well, sometimes I miss being touched you know? Even if it's just a hug."

My mother holding my hand on that hot day brought up this recollection. And this recollection took me down a rabbit hole of inane thoughts.

Is this my responsibility now? To be my mother's TOUCHER? I wondered. *OK, OK, I'll have to rearrange some things, but OK, she **did** birth me.*

What is WRONG with you? She's your mother for Christ's sake. She's just being affectionate.

Yeah, but it's a bit much. Plus it's hot.

You're a bit much.

I mean, what if people think we're lesbians?! We're the same height, and from a distance we don't look far apart in age...

You are ridiculous.

It was an absurd churn, a churn that made me feel like an awful, selfish daughter. As we exited the cemetery, we stopped to gaze at a large, framed photo that used to hang in the entrance corridor. It showed JFK and Jackie in the back of the presidential limo moments before he was shot that day in Dallas. Texas Governor John Connally and his wife are pictured in front of them. All are smiling, oblivious.

I noticed a woman and her mother standing just ahead of us, to the left. They looked to be about the same age as my mom and me. The daughter looked posh, wearing a crisp white T-shirt with a scarf, tasteful but sexy shorts, and medium-length blondish-brown hair pulled back into a low ponytail.

"What's that photo of?" the mother asked her daughter.

The daughter turned toward her for full effect: "What are you, *RETARDED?* It's JFK! Before he was shot!" Her mother, shorter and less trendy than her daughter, looked a little embarrassed but otherwise shrugged it off.

A line in the sand was drawn. Before this moment: innocence. After this moment: knowledge that I lived in a world where family members referred to each other as retards.

You know what, I'm a fine daughter, I thought.

But it was an eye-opener regarding my willingness to be intimate. Back then if a guy looked me in the eyes for more than two seconds, I would either look away or pat him on the back and say, "OK, that's enough now," in a tone that sounded as condescending as you think. I was just beginning to realize I was unhappy and still making unhealthy choices. I was moderately exercising—I played in a volleyball and football league at least twice per week—but I was not eating a good diet, I was drinking a *lot,* and I was rarely at home because I didn't want to be left alone with that negative self-talk. My cats, themselves unhappy with my frequent absences, let me know it by pissing in my laundry, so for a few months I smelled faintly of pee. It was time to get happy, and to do that I needed to open myself up. To open myself up, I needed help.

"Talk to me about what's going on," my therapist said at the beginning of our first appointment.

"I'm good!"

"You mentioned on the phone that you recently went through a divorce and a fresh breakup. How are you feeling about all that today?"

"Really good!"

"Great," she said, "but since, you know, you're *here*…why don't you just…*talk…*"

At first I tried to trick my therapist into thinking I didn't really need it—that I was, in fact, holding it together quite well considering the circumstances. I was thriving at work, had terrific friends, and didn't smell like cat pee anymore. I was completely well adjusted and just needed her to validate that for me, and I'd be on my way.

"My God, you're *better* than good," she'd say. "You're *perfect!* Can I use you in a case study? Perfect Patient X?"

Sticking your head in the sand is easy. Doing the work to be who you want to be is not. Gently but surely she helped me begin to examine my life and put it into context: to see patterns where I didn't and rationale where I couldn't. We set goals. I was getting somewhere. In a few months I was able to identify the behaviors and types of relationships I didn't want to continue. From there I just needed a plan to transition from who I was to who I wanted to be. But who was *that?*

At least once per month my mom and I would meet for dinner and sometimes a movie. She belonged to a film club that gave its members access to advance screenings a few weeks before they were distributed nationally. One was *Chocolat* starring Juliette Binoche. She played Vianne, a free-spirited drifter and single mother to a six-year-old daughter. Following the wind, they'd move from place to place, settling temporarily somewhere until things got boring or hard, and then it was time to move again. In the movie, Vianne and her daughter arrive in a small, rural town in France and open a chocolate shop during Lent: a metaphor for temptation. While the town's small-minded mayor labels Vianne a temptress, she is also seen as a helper to various townsfolk. She is compassionate, clever, and strong. But can she resist the wind the next time it blows through? Can she save herself?

"I want to be Vianne!" I said to my mom as we exited the theater.

"Juliette Binoche? I know, isn't she just luminous?"

"Not Juliette Binoche, VIANNE."

I was almost thirty, had never lived outside of Ohio, and had barely traveled beyond touristy locales. Vianne made me want to wander. I had closed myself off from real intimacy to avoid future hurt. Vianne made me want to see the good in people, to be kind, and to connect in a meaningful way. Vianne made me want to both chase the wind but also trust my instincts when they told me to let it pass.

"I want to be Vianne," I said again, for good measure.

A couple months before, I started working with Lyndsey, a senior consultant out of my firm's New York office, who became a real mentor. She pulled me into projects in Boston, NYC, Atlanta, Houston, and Washington, DC, where she made a permanent move. Soon, I was traveling to the nation's capitol twice per month and staying for three to four days. After about six months of this, we were at dinner when she said, "Why don't you just move here?"

"Yeah, right." It had never occurred to me to leave Cleveland. Not even once.

"Jen, where did you go to college?"

"University of Toledo."

"So, you've never left Ohio?"

"I went to London once. AND Chicago AND New York City... remember?"

"Jen, when I was fifteen, I said to my parents, 'When I am eighteen, I'm leaving Ohio and never coming back!' You're, um, twenty-nine?"

"So?"

"So, there's a job opening under me in the DC office, and I want you to take it."

Over the next few days, I channeled Vianne.

"Qu'est-ce que vous dit votre cœur, ma chère?" she lilted to me.

"My heart says to go."

"Ensuite, il doit être," she replied. *Then it must be.*

I put in the application and began telling people of my plans. My friends were completely supportive, but my parents made counter-arguments for staying in Cleveland.

"Washington is a stupid city," said my mom at first.

"Mom, it's not stupid."

"Yes, it is. It's dangerous." Hey, she didn't want me to leave. She pulled out the tactics she thought would work. My dad, who has a love for Cleveland that dare not speak its name, applied a more pragmatic approach.

"Halle Berry's from Cleveland," he said.

My stepmother piped up, "The Indians are doing great!"

"Yeah, I know guys." I smiled. I knew why they were doing it. They liked having my sister and me around to go to dinner with or to see movies. We were their buddies. But eventually, they got behind the move.

I hardly knew anyone when I first arrived, so random conversations became a way for me to socialize and learn about the city, which is rich in culture and much, much more than the federal government. One night, late, I hailed a cab in DC, heading home. A yellow cab pulled over with two dark-skinned men sitting in the front seat. Both appeared to be about seventy years old.

"He is a friend who is with me on my last ride," said the driver after he pulled up to greet me. "Is that OK?"

"Sure," I said and got into the cab. "Where are you from?"

"Eritrea. Do you know where that is?"

"Near Ethiopia, right?"

"Impressive!" they exclaimed in an affectionately chiding manner.

"When did you move here?" I asked. The friend started talking. He said that he was given a student visa when he was eighteen and soon fell in love with an American Caucasian woman his age. She loved him too, but her parents didn't want her dating a black man. He overheard them say so when she brought him home for dinner and they thought he was in the bathroom. They broke up, his student visa expired, and so he returned to Eritrea. After a couple years, he married and had children. And then ten years later he got a call from the woman he had loved in the states. He was surprised to hear from her, and she explained that she had always kept him in her heart. She had flown to Eritrea on a whim to see him. He explained he was married and that he couldn't see her, and so they chatted by phone for about an hour, catching up on old times.

"And then what happened?" I asked from the edge of my backseat in the cab.

"Well, that gesture stuck with me. I returned to the states years later to visit family and friends, and I thought about her. I found her mother's number in the phone book and called. She remembered me and put me in touch with her daughter."

"Oh my God, did you meet up with her?" I asked. "My place is over here. Tell me the rest!"

"We agreed to meet up at a train station, and she was there before me, waiting on the platform."

"Yeah? What were you thinking at that moment?"

Silence. *How sweet,* I thought. *He's searching for the right words...*

"That she was very ugly!" his friend, the driver, said and then started to laugh.

"It's true, she was," he said also laughing, and then he shrugged. "Still, we had a very nice lunch."

I laughed all the way up to my front door. I wasn't laughing at the woman in the story. I actually felt for her. I was laughing because you never know how a story is going to turn out. These random encounters warmed me and made me realize how easy it can be to connect—even briefly.

I want to be like Vianne.

When you're opening yourself up, even everyday things can seem profound, like the Metro. I cannot underestimate the influence the Metro had on my decision to move. To me, subways meant big city, important city, cool city. After I moved and first started riding as *a local,* I beamed with pure joy. *I live in a place with a subway!* I'd think. *I'm a big city girl!* I'd smile at the other people during the morning and evening commutes, but they just gave me strange looks or ignored me completely. Soon, I acclimated and became just another rider who stared off vacantly while listening to my iPod. But for a while, I still felt that joy.

I traveled a lot to other parts of the country, both for pleasure and for work. A couple weeks after I moved, I traveled to a client site in Houston. On the leg back, I went up to the ticket counter to get my boarding pass.

"Where you headed, sweetheart?" the attendant asked as I handed her my ID.

"Cleveland."

"Hmmm…" she said while ticking away at the keyboard. "I don't have you booked on a flight to Cleveland. I have you booked on a flight to *Washington, DC*...." She raised her cadence at the end in a sort of half question, so as not to insult me.

"Oh, right! I live in DC now!"

She laughed. "Hey, it's easy to forget where you're going sometimes."

I thought about how strange it was that I had forgotten. As we approached National Airport, I could see the monuments all lit up against the night, their reflections swaying in the Potomac River, and I leaned my head against the window and smiled.
"No one really knows you here," Vianne said to me as the plane began its sharp descent. "You are free from your old life."

Free to be you and me.

ROAD TRIP

"Are you on drugs?"

My dad and stepmom asked me this as we sat across their kitchen table. I had just announced that I would be taking a leave of absence from work. I was going to live in Amsterdam—possibly for up to a year—and travel around Europe. Other than that I had no real plan. It reminded me of the scene from *The Graduate* in which Benjamin tells his parents of his plans to win back his love, Elaine, who'd rejected him after it was revealed that he'd slept with her mother, Mrs. Robinson.

Benjamin's Father: "Ben, this whole idea sounds pretty half-baked."
Benjamin: "Oh, it's not. It's completely baked."

Dave and I met the year before, not long after I moved to DC. He was a bartender at a popular place, and one afternoon I stopped in with a friend and ordered a Guinness. He poured it properly—stopping when the glass was half full and waiting for it to settle before filling the rest, but he forgot the second part.

"Can I get you anything?" he asked a few minutes later, noticing I didn't have a drink in front of me.

"Yeah, my *beer,*" I said as I directed my eyes to the half-filled pint glass. He laughed and we talked for a few minutes. He was in his midtwenties, a little taller than me, and slim with broad shoulders, and he had a beautiful face that was already wrinkled from laughing.

The following Tuesday night, I returned to the same place with a friend. It was packed. A few seconds in, I spotted Dave behind the bar, and he waved.

"Who's that?" my friend asked.

"Him? I met him on Saturday. You know, I thought there was some flirty banter going back and forth, but I'm surprised he remembered me." We sat down at a high-top table, and Dave approached us.

"What can I get you?" he asked.

"Well," I said, thinking I was being sexy/cool, "I'd tell you, but I'm not sure I can trust you to remember it."

"I'm sorry, did we meet...?" and then he let the question hang there.

My friend started laughing. "Oh, that's...sorry..." followed by more laughing. "She thought you were waving to her...She thought you two had a *moment...*"

I shot her a look, but he just looked confused. As it turned out, he was waving to someone behind me.

"Anyway, I'll have a gin and tonic," I said quickly. He didn't forget me after that, and following some choice stolen glances throughout the night, he asked for my number. He was sweet and sexy and didn't think I was a slut when I dry humped him on his couch after our first date. We started hanging out a couple times a week, sometimes just watching movies, sometimes out.

Hey, I like where this is going.

Me too.

I was thinking of visiting friends in Europe for New Year's, and my friend Angela offered up her place in Amsterdam as a possible stop. She would be on the beach somewhere in Thailand with her boyfriend, Neil.

"It's all yours," she said.

It was late November, and Dave and I were out to dinner. We had been dating six weeks when I blurted out:

"Do you want to go to Amsterdam with me for New Year's?" We hadn't even ordered our meals. *Why did I just ask him that?*

"Yes," he said. We spent the rest of the meal excitedly planning the trip. Amsterdam-Paris-Amsterdam-Home. Ten days. We arrived in the Netherlands on December 29, and friends of mine flew in from London to meet us (he charmed them). Skinny, blond Dutch girls aggressively flirted with him in bars (he didn't respond). I got jealous (he reassured me). It was all going so well, and the trip had just started.

Paris.

We took the train from Amsterdam and arrived at our hotel in the St. Germain Arrondissement at around 9:30 p.m. We dropped our bags, bundled up, and set out into the cold streets, which were dark save for the streetlights. Dave stopped me in the middle of our walk and leaned me against a wall. He looked at me...in my eyes, at my forehead, back to my eyes, and then at my lips before he leaned in and kissed me. Then he tucked me into him and directed me forward. Seconds later, we rounded the corner, and there she was, the Eiffel Tower. We powered toward it, love drunk, as if it were the North Star, and once we reached it, we turned around and walked back, stopping in at various places for warmth and drink.

Sufficiently intoxicated, we went back to our hotel, flopped in the bed, and held each other in the dark. I was feeling it—all that gushy muck—but instead of saying, "Hey, I'm really digging this trip with you," I said, "I love you."

"Oh, that's so nice. Thank you." He stroked my hair, smiled and me, and didn't pull away. "I think you're great. I'm having the best time." *Well, fantastic!*

Within ten minutes he was snoring, so I went to sleep too. *Deal with it tomorrow, deal with it tomorrow.*

The next morning I woke up with a cracking hangover: severe head pain and extreme dehydration. I went into the bathroom and downed a glass of water and then stepped gingerly into the shower. I lost myself in the warm water for a few moments before my eyes shot open.

"Fuck!" *You told him you loved him last night. And he didn't say it back.* At the realization, all I wanted to do was get out of there. I wrapped a towel around me and saw that Dave was still passed out. I shook him lightly.

"Hmmm..?"

"Hey, I'm going to go to the Louvre. Do you want to come?"

"Uhn uhn…"

"I'll take that as a no. OK, I'll see you later."

"I'll be waiting for you..." And then he fell back into unconsciousness.

Once coffee and croissants were inside me I felt revived and grateful for time by myself. Instead of spending the day obsessing, wondering what he thought, I could spend the day diverting myself with paintings and sculptures and costumes and history. Someone once told me that if you spent thirty seconds viewing each piece of art in that museum, it would take you two and a half years to go through the museum. I don't know if that's true, but I do know that there is no better distraction from an errant "I love you" than a trip through the Louvre.

I walked back to the hotel in a dreamy state and saw Dave sitting at a table outside with a carafe of wine. I sat down next to him, nervous, and the waiter brought over another glass.

"How was it?" Dave smiled without a hint of discomfort as he poured.

"Amazing. There was this one piece..." and there we were back in the swing. We didn't talk about it for the rest of the trip nor soon after that, and I'd be lying if I said it didn't nag me.

"I mean, at some point, I'm making an ass of myself, right?" I asked my friend Claire. "At some point, I'm the girl who waits around thinking I'll get an 'I love you' when in reality I get an e-mail that says, 'Hey, got back together with my old girlfriend. I think you're great, though, and hope we can stay friends!' right?"

"Not necessarily," Claire said.

"Yeah, right."

"Think of it this way…If those three words didn't exist, if they were just…obliterated from our vocabulary, would you be happy with the way things are?"

"Well, yes…"

"OK then."

I'd *try* to be patient and I'd *try* to be strong, but that's not so easy for a person who is oceans of emotions but always wants to appear in control. Sometimes it gets the better of me.

"Why haven't you told me you loved me?" I asked one night in frustration, while we were lying in his bed trying to fall asleep. He was silent for a moment, thoughtful.

"Give me time, I will."

"When?" I demanded.

"I'm just not as fast as you are, Jen. It's not that I don't feel it; it's just that, you know, I got out of a six-year relationship six weeks before I met you. I just want to make sure it's right."

"But I feel like an asshole," I said.

He laughed and kissed me on the head. "I promise you, I'll get there. What's not to love?"

About a month later, he made good on his promise, and about a month after that, my friend Angela called to tell me her apartment in Amsterdam would be empty as she was moving to London to give it a go with her boyfriend. Would we like to use it for a while before she put it on sale? We did not hesitate: yes.

Dave and I notified our employers, and they agreed to hold our positions until we returned, even though we didn't know when that would be. We took on second jobs to save up for the trip: Dave found another bartending gig, and I worked as a waitress in a sports bar that became a nightclub after the games were broadcast. It wasn't awesome: the manager was schizophrenic, people were drinking *Leaving Las Vegas* style, and the men got a little grabby sometimes. Still, I met a great friend working there, it was a few blocks from our apartment, and I cleared about $500 per week on top of what I made from my full-time salary. We moved in together. We saved a lot of money. We were a team.

I began to imagine a life with Dave. Not as a married couple. I didn't want the expectations, the blatant *trap* of marriage. I wanted to be Kurt and Goldie. Oprah and Steadman. Bert and Ernie. But never, ever married.

"Are you on drugs?" my dad asked when I first relayed the plan. "The economy is slowing down, and you don't know for sure if they'll hold your jobs."

My dad and stepmom hadn't traveled much, nor were they particularly interested in other cultures, so me being on drugs was of course the only explanation for such arresting stuff.

"Dad, just because Amsterdam has coffee houses doesn't mean I'm addicted to drugs." I was annoyed. Here I was successful, healthy, and on the road to happy. I had a well-thought-out plan, complete with risk mitigation strategies, and they dare question my extracurricular activities? Who *cares* if I was on drugs? It was obviously working!

But I wasn't asking for their permission, only for their blessing, which I got right before we left.

Dave traveled back to Cleveland with me two weeks before the trip and stayed at my mom's the first night. She called me into the kitchen before dinner, leaving him in the living room. She was stirring a pot on the stove and beckoned me to her, all *Mission Impossible* style. I gathered up close.

"Yessss....?"

"Dave just asked if he could marry you in Europe," she said, looking around the corner. "Isn't that amazing?"

"Mom!" I whisper-yelled. "Don't you think those would have been the first words out of my mouth if *I knew that*? He obviously wants that to be a surprise!" I watched as the realization spread across her face. But she was so raw in her happiness that I decided to let it pass, and we hugged.

I was shocked, however, and went into an obsessive-compulsive churn. *How do I bring this up? He's in the middle of asking for my hand! What made him so sure? Isn't he worried I'll say no? He knows how I feel about marriage! What WILL I say? Shouldn't I know the answer to that question?!? AHHH!*

The next morning, I called my dad to alert them to Dave's intentions. I needed to prepare him because he cannot keep a happy secret. He wears it on his face and looks like he will burst within five seconds—which he usually does—but it's so out of place and vague you're left more confused than anything else. I figured he could use a few hours to get it out of his system.

"Whatever your instinct, do the opposite!" I suggested brightly. This was actually the worst thing I could do because then I started getting *involved.*

"I'll be leaving the room for approximately twelve minutes," I'd say at various intervals of the visit and run upstairs randomly throughout the day. By the fourth time, Dave had done the deed, and I came down and sat at the table.

"We said yes!" said my dad.

Dave whipped his head around to my father, confused. I raised my eyebrows and gave my dad the knife-sliding-across-the-throat gesture and said, "So…what movie should we see?" That night Dave and I were making out on the couch when I just couldn't bear to keep the secret.

"My parents sold you out," I said.

"What?" He tried to sit up fast and disentangle himself from me. I didn't let go.

"Yeah, my mom slipped it…"

"Wait? You knew *yesterday…?"*

"It was by mistake, and I thought we'd have one more shot with the big guy," I said, pointing in the direction of my dad's bedroom. "I'm really sorry, sweetheart. I know that's not the way you wanted it to go down, but they didn't do it because they don't want it to happen. They did it because they're excited." I realized that with Dave I was becoming less sarcastic, more authentic. He softened me.

"I wanted to do an actual proposal while in Europe, after we got there."

"I know, it sucks. But you still can. You can still surprise me."

It was encouragement but also a stalling tactic. I didn't want to lose him, but I also didn't want to get married.

We kissed until our lips began to blister.

Dave and I arrived in Amsterdam with six full bags of luggage. We took the tram from the airport to our neighborhood of Leidseplein. The square was pulsing with people and shops and bars and restaurants and trams and bikes. We threw our belongings in Angela's apartment and rushed out to take it in, practically skipping through the city, hand in hand, until the jet lag grabbed hold.

During the first two weeks, we felt invisible on the crowded streets compared to the Dutch who seemed so tall. We went to museums and packed picnics and read in Vondel Park. We sat in outdoor cafés sipping Heineken and Witte beers while we watched street performers mime, bounce soccer balls endlessly, and dance on ropes in nude slings that made them look naked while climbing.

In Leidseplein

Then we took off.

Normandy, France.
Dave arranged for us to first stay at the Ferme de Marcelet, a farmhouse owned by Solange and Pierre, a couple in their sixties. The house and surrounding structures were made of brick in varying shades of tan and gray. Plants and grass and hedges surrounded the property, which included cows, a newborn calf, and a peacock that strutted around and screamed. In the morning, we gorged ourselves on warm bread and jam and butter before exploring Bayeaux.

For Dave, a history buff, the focal point of the trip was the beaches. We were there on the fifty-eighth anniversary of D-Day. We walked around Gold Beach, Omaha, Juno, and Pointe du hoc. We peered through bunkers and went to gravesites. We imagined the kids who had to fight, particularly the Americans who had approached from the water that day. Sitting targets, but huge in number. A reporter we met said he had talked to a German soldier who returned for the remembrance. The soldier recalled the sun rising on June 6, 1944. As he began to make out the fleet of tiny boats zooming toward shore, he turned to his bunker mate and said, "We just lost the war."

We talked to many people who fought that day from America and the United Kingdom, including a Welshman named Bill Evans, who planted a huge, wet, three-second kiss on my lips before saying good-bye. I looked at Dave.

"Ah well," he said with a shrug. "He *is* a veteran." I wiped my mouth on my sleeve.

On the way back to Amsterdam we stopped in Rouen, where Joan of Arc was burned at the stake at nineteen. She was a peasant convinced she heard messages from God and wound up leading the French Army to victory during the Hundred Years' War. After a few hours, we headed north, Dave driving and me navigating as we listened to our worn out copy of the *Moulin Rouge* soundtrack. In the summer, Holland stays light until ten or eleven. We arrived when the sun was setting amid colors of pale blues, purples, and pinks, his hand over mine, his thumb caressing my ring finger.

Interlaken/Zermatt, Switzerland.

We had barely unpacked the bags from our last trip when we decided to drive to Interlaken, Switzerland, which was a little over fourteen hours from Amsterdam by car. We packed snacks, maps, and travel books and practiced Swiss-German phrases.

"Wo häts en Chübel, es Grosses?"

"Yes, probably the most important phrase." *Where can I find a large glass of beer?*

We drove on the Autobahn. Though we were moving at a swift pace, we often had to move quickly to the right lane to make way for numerous Mercedes cars that whizzed past, giving the appearance that their wheels barely touched the ground. We arrived late at night in Interlaken, which translates as *between lakes* — in this case Lake Brienz to the east and Lake Thun to the west. It was dark and quiet and fairytale-like as we drove around the water into town.

We woke up in the early morning just as the fog was lifting from the mountains and drank kaffee and ate pastries outside. Suitably charged we headed to the Jungfrau region and climbed and hiked and refreshed ourselves in the natural springs that surrounded us. We watched people base jump out of small planes, and we discovered Trummelbach Falls, a connected system of ten illuminated glacial waterfalls in the mountains. We fell more in love.

On the night of the Fourth of July we headed to the Funny Farm, a hostel set up to promote partying and hookups. There was the Space Camp pool area with trees and lights and room to lounge with our drinks. There was the Guinness tent, which served my favorite beer. The bathrooms were pitch black with disco balls hanging from the ceiling. DJs were playing tunes, and the smell of weed drifted under our noses. We decided to split up and find the source among the one hundred or so people ten years younger than us on average. I introduced myself to a group of nineteen- to twenty-year-olds, and a young woman struck up a conversation with me.

"Are you traveling with your boyfriend?" she asked.

"Yes."

"Oh my God, what's that like? Because I'm traveling with friends, and my boyfriend is back home, and he's super jealous, like worried that I'm going to kiss someone, and you know what? I already have! But who cares? I'm nineteen, and if I want to kiss someone while I'm traveling through Europe, I mean, I should, right?"

"Totally…"

At this point a boy of about twenty, who was clearly wasted, sat down beside me, took my hand, and stared at my face, smiling. He didn't say a word. I wanted to go. *Where is Dave?* I went looking for him, and the boy followed, holding on to my shirt as I dragged him around.

I found Dave talking to a Dutch guy in the Guinness tent. "Yeah," he said to the guy as I approached. "I know what you mean. But when you really think about it, you only cheat on someone you don't really want to be with anyway. I mean, that's how I felt about an ex-girlfriend…"

"Wait," I interrupted. "You cheated on a girlfriend?"

"Well, yeah, but not really…Wait who's that?" he asked, referring to the mute twenty-year-old holding my hand.

"Him? I don't know! Don't change the subject!" The Dutch guy looked uncomfortable.

"Jen, I was twenty! I was immature…It's not like I would do that *now.*"

"Or don't you mean *yet?*" I stomped off, and when my appendage didn't disengage, I led him to some tables by the tent and said, "Stay here!" before going to the pool area to pout. Dave found me a few minutes later.

"You're being a little sensitive, don't you think?"

"Can we just go?"

We walked in silence back to our hotel. *Once a cheater, always a cheater,* I thought. But I knew it was a misdirection, a way to avoid thinking and talking about THE FEAR. *Don't you mean once burned, twice shy?*

I also knew my irritation was rooted in the vague plans for our elope-ment, which was targeted for Italy in late September. I was sure I wanted to be with Dave, but I wasn't sure he was fully cooked. He had been in a long-term relationship as well as had his fair share of short-term flings (at the bar they called him "The Kid," as in, "Back in the day, 'The Kid' used to score some hot ass!") He had trav-eled extensively, and we had the same values. These were pros; I didn't want to be with someone with whom I wasn't compatible or who would look back one day and think, *I haven't lived.* But he was also comfortable with prolonged periods without structure, and I was not. He didn't like dealing with budgets or spending. He began looking for ways to extend our stay in Europe indefinitely. I was al-ready thinking of what life would look like when we returned to the states and whether it would be different *if* we returned as a married couple. I thought about all of this as we walked in silence.

"I don't want to get married," I said to him once we were in our pri-vate hostel bed, pretending to sleep. I was lying on my side with my back turned to him. He turned on the light.

"Why?"

"Because. Things will change. You don't think they will, but they do. The person you were in love with becomes the person you no longer even *like*. And when that happens, you'll feel *caged*…"

"I will not feel 'caged' with you."

"You will, at some point you will, and when you do, we'll find new ways to hurt each other. Then you'll meet some willing girl at the bar and…"

"I'm not your ex-husband. I'm not going to do that to you. I want to *marry* you. I've never wanted to marry *anyone*, but I want to marry *you*. Doesn't that mean something?"

I rolled over and faced him, snuggling up close so as much of our naked skin was touching as possible.

"*You* mean everything. Marriage means *shit.*" My God *was* I a Nicholas Sparks character? I mean, I didn't have a disease nor was I involved in a mystery of any sort (that I *knew of*…bum bum bum). I just didn't want to repeat mistakes, because repeating them would make me question my judgment, deeply, and if I came out the other side with the notion that I was flawed, I would slide on some of the progress I'd made. *Better to be risk averse*, I thought, even though I loved him and even though I was committed to it *like* a marriage. Wasn't that enough?

"Well, it's not 'shit' to me, Jen, but OK, I won't pressure you."

"What do we do about the wedding date in Italy?"

"Let's just keep it on the books. If you want to cancel, we'll cancel."

The next morning we made the trek from Interlaken to Zermatt. It was only forty-six miles away but required us to go up and then down a large mountain range by car, so it took hours. I had to will myself to stay calm as Dave drove the narrow road (with no guard-rails!) beside sharp, ten-thousand-foot drops into the spectacular, snow-covered mountains to our right.

"Don't look down," I cautioned.

"Well, now that's the only thing I want to do!" But he kept his hands firmly planted at ten and two. At the top of the range, we saw a chalet and decided to stop for lunch. It was two-thirds full, with about twenty-five people scattered among the tables. We looked at the menu and decided on cheese fondue for two. When we ordered, the waitress started smiling and giggling, but we didn't know why. When she brought out the bubbling cauldron of Gruyere, everyone started laughing and clapping as they burst into song. We sat frozen, unsure of what to do. They continued clapping while we politely smiled then stared at us until we speared our first piece of bread and dipped it in. After that they went back to their meals. Being far from fluent in Swiss-German, we never did get an explanation. But we didn't care. Our bellies were full of cheese. When we arrived in Zermatt, we took a cable ride toward the top of the range where it was cold and snowy and walked around for about two hours, exuberant and ready to keep going.

Back in Amsterdam, a more organized life began to emerge. We met a delightful girl from New York City in the middle of Leidseplein, Michelle, who was promoting an American improv comedy troupe called Boom Chicago. She was from the states, taking graduate classes and reading *Ulysses* for fun. She was bubbly and laughed easily but could immediately turn serious.

"This one time, my mom was in the grocery store, and this guy in front of her tried to pay his tab with rocks," she said, cracking up. "My mom wanted to pay for his food, but he seemed so earnest that she thought it would insult him."

"What did the cashier say?" I asked.

She looked at me stoned-faced. "I don't know. I didn't think that story needed a punch line." This made me howl, and she turned away from me to distribute more materials for the Boom shows.

"Hey," Dave said to her, "how did you start doing that?"

"This?" she asked, pointing to the materials she was holding. "Oh, it was easy. I just went into the ticket counter and told them I wanted to be a promoter. These leaflets are guides to the city. That's how I draw them in. 'Free guide to the city!' Once I start talking to them I say, 'and there's also this great comedy show tonight—if you take this guide into the ticket booth, you'll get a discount.'"

She pointed to a white square on the back cover with a stamp. "See this? That's my stamp. When people turn this in, the ticket person logs it according to the stamp. Then we meet once per week as a group and get our commissions in cash."

"Really?" I said.

"Yeah. And it's soooo easy to sell. After a few days of walking around and getting stoned, the Brits and Americans—especially the couples—are ready for some passive entertainment. I just smoke some weed and head out for a few hours whenever I want and enjoy the sunshine and talk to people."

Dave and I looked at each other. "I can easily get you in," she said and soon she did.

It gave us some spending money and a lot of free entertainment, because that troupe was mad talented. We got to hang with Jordan Peele *(MADtv, Key & Peele)*, Ike Barinholz *(Eastbound & Down, The Mindy Project),* and Nicole Parker *(MADtv)* who were there during that time.

Dave continued the mixed martial arts training he was devoted to back home, and I decided to sign up for ten Muay Thai kickboxing classes thinking, *I've done Tae Bo, so this will be like that, right?* No. No, it was not.

The program was intense, with a thirty-minute warm-up that nearly made me puke a few times on its own, followed by instruction, then sparring. My body, which was accustomed to light jogs on the treadmill and strength training using five-pound weights was about to be tested. We had shin guards and gloves only. No face guards. During instruction, we'd pair up, and my partners would punch and kick with force much harder than I anticipated. When we sparred, no one held back. This wasn't an aerobic exercise class, I quickly surmised. People were training here. *To be fighters.* My first couple weeks, I simply dodged and weaved as best I could, and when I tried to throw punches, I looked like a cat playfully pawing at a string. The instructor was Dutch-Surinamese Muay Thai World Champion Ivan Hippolyte, and he took a special interest in me.

After a few classes, he said, "How are you liking it?"

"I like it. But it's really hard."

"You will get the hang of it. You have it in you. Push your body. I will help you." I'd like to think that if I didn't have huge breasts and a pretty face he'd have offered that anyway, but I'm no fool. Still, I took him up on it. I liked the idea of pushing my body. I hadn't done that before.

Me and Ivan.

"You will?"

"Yes, after classes, when I have breaks, I will work with you."

"Do I have to pay you?"

He laughed. "No." I decided to buy a thirty-class package and see what I could do. I got better. I met with Ivan, who spent thirty minutes after class with me drilling me on moves. My body started changing and becoming more toned. I was getting stronger.

I met women, one in particular named Kim, who was really generous with me and encouraged me from the get-go.

"Kick from the back position. You'll get more power that way," she'd say in her Dutch accent, and, "Good, good, that's it," when I got it right.

The place smelled of sweat and cleaning supplies and was brightly lit. It contained a bright blue mat as flooring and mirrors or glass for walls. At the front of the training area was a weight room where huge men with shaved heads and several tattoos lifted hundreds of pounds. The gloves and shin guards had a funk so foul from encasing hundreds of different hands and legs that I swiftly decided to invest in my own. I liked going to the 8:00 p.m. classes because it coincided with Dave's training schedule. For a girl who liked her alone time, I was discovering I didn't mind spending endless hours with him. In fact, I missed him whenever we were apart, which was hardly ever. We'd arrive home at around the same time and shower. Then we'd eat dinner, sometimes smoke a joint, and zone out in front of the television, fighting sleep so we could spend more awake time together. Oh, but we were deliciously tired those nights.

There was another element to the eight o'clock classes, and that was the predominance of men in attendance. There were many times when I was the only woman, and I wanted to look like a contender, not only for myself, but also for my sparring partner. I didn't want any of them to think, *Great. Got stuck with the girl.* Sometimes I'd get in good blows, and the guys would light up, pleasantly surprised. Sometimes I'd do that, and the guys would get angry and hit harder than necessary. One time a guy kicked me in the head, and I went *down.* Another time I surprised a guy with a hard roundhouse to his side. His face grew dark, and he retaliated by punching me so hard in the stomach that I fell to the floor and crab crawled backward until I was against the wall and could catch my wind. Ivan came over and immediately bent down.

"Are you OK?"

I nodded. He yelled at my opponent and then turned to look at me again. I waved him off and stayed against the wall, watching the others spar, until I slowly regained my breath. I took the tram home, and when I arrived I burst into tears. Dave sat me down, but it took ten minutes for me to tell the story because I was catching up on all the crying I had held in when I was at the gym.

"I don't know if I want to go back," I said. As with the marriage decision, he left this one up to me.

Summer in Amsterdam was beautiful, and we could view its bounty at bloemenmarkts and other outdoor vendors. Shopkeepers in our local neighborhood were at first cold but polite. After seeing us regularly for a couple months, they welcomed us warmly.

"Goedemorgen!" they'd greet us. "Hoe gaat het?" *How are you?*

"Goed, dank u vel. En met you?" *And you?*

"Ah. Life is gezellig…" *Gezellig* was one of my two favorite Dutch words. It is an adverb with no English translation, but it can mean cozy or fun or content depending on the circumstances. My other favorite word was *lekker*, which roughly translates as delicious. We heard it a lot in Holland. "This meal is lekker," or "Did you see that girl's ass? It's lekker."

Twice between July and August, we traveled to London to visit our friends Angela, Neil, and Claire and walk around the city. Dave's arm seemed to be permanently draped over my shoulder. He kissed me constantly on the cheek and looked lovingly at me across many, many bottles of wine.

"Jen," he said one night at dinner, "I know you haven't made up your mind about getting married, but I need you to know…in the long-term, it's a deal breaker if you don't."

This was new information. "But why?"

"Because of what it means to me. It means that you chose me; that we chose each other. It means security…"

"No it doesn't," I cut in. "Marriage is *no* guarantee, and statistically speaking…"

"It's not scientific," he said, looking down at the menu. "It's how I feel."

Jen, do not let him go.

Italy.
Our wedding date was scheduled for September 24 in Positano, Italy, but we arrived in the country two weeks earlier. We had disagreements about where we should venture. Dave wanted to visit Lake Como, and I wanted to go to Venice. Dave wanted to roam in Tuscany, and I wanted to go to Florence. Dave thought of places as eternal and therefore eternally available. I thought of them more fleetingly. *What if I'm never here again?*

So Venice won out, but so did Tuscany.

We walked through the Venetian streets and window-shopped. We caught a performing arts preview with opera and ballet in the Piazza San Marco, with lights twinkling from both the electronics and the stars. And then we took a ride through the canals. Our young gondolier spoke slowly and with a heavy accent: "On the left-a is-a the castle of the great-a lover, Cassanova…"

When we docked, Dave got down on one knee and proposed. I didn't think of fear. All I though was, *…and his heart was going like mad and yes I said yes I will Yes*[5]. An American flag flapped softly in the distance in honor of the one-year anniversary of 9/11.

---

5   From Molly Bloom's Soliloquy, *Ulysses*, James Joyce

Dave's birthday was the next day, so I surprised him with breakfast in bed that I cobbled together from the continental breakfast in the lobby. I found a candle and placed it in a muffin. We took off for Tuscany with no agenda other than to find a place to stay, and find one we did. We stumbled upon the Gargonza Castili, a castle that has huge rooms for one hundred dollars per night and a gourmet restaurant. The grounds alone were worth the stay. There were olive and fig trees and grape vines and forests and rolling hills. Our room was all dark wooden beams and sandy stonework. There was a private fireplace set with kindling, papers, and matches.

We went to festivals and ate crazy-delicious pasta for two euros or stayed quiet on the Gargonza grounds, sipping wine in one of the many private alcoves designed for such pursuits. After three nights we headed to Rome and continued to get high on the food, which was simple and sublime. I was surprised when we came out of a Metro stop and boom! There was the Coliseum right across the street. I expected it to be more protected, harder to get to. But I suppose much of my imagination was attracted to what went on *inside* the structure. I hadn't thought much about the outside. We toured the Vatican and tipped our sunglasses to the Swiss guards. "We've had your cheese."

We headed to the Amalfi Coast and settled in a small apartment compound in Sorrento that smelled of lemon groves. Finally we got cracking on planning the wedding. Others in the compound were taken with our plans, and because we were so relaxed, they took on our stress for us.

"Have you chosen your dress yet?" they asked. "Your flowers?"

"No."

"AH! What are you waiting for, child?"

Dave's parents met us in Italy. We had planned a vacation with them in that region, and, coincidentally, it was the only place we could get legally married as Americans, so they served as our proud witnesses. My parents called us the night before and blew kisses through the phone. We were not nervous. We exchanged vows at the Italian equivalent of the justice of the peace at 2:00 p.m. on a veranda in Positano that overlooked the cliffs sliding into the Mediterranean.

We celebrated with totani e patate, a calamari dish with potato and cherry tomatoes, pasta with sea clams, and chocolate almond cake from Capri. Then we checked into the honeymoon suite at a hotel in Ravello and barely left the hotel for two days.

On the way back to Amsterdam, we went to Brussels and stood still for several minutes in front of Jacques-Louis David's *Death of Marat* and marveled at a gallery's worth of Bruegels. Amsterdam was colder than we had left it, and with money dwindling, we decided we'd return to the states in December. With an expiration date announced, we had a steady stream of visitors from October to November, including my mom, Dave's brother, and friends. We joined them to partake in all of the touristy things we hadn't yet done and some we had (like the amazing museums). We walked around the Red Light District and saw a sex show, which was clinical and choreographed and rarely sexy. It had an air of performance art, so I spit out my drink when a friend said, "It's like Cirque de Soliel, but with *fucking*."

After Thanksgiving the last of our friends left, taking some of our things with them to lessen our load on the way back. We spent the last couple weeks saying personal good-byes to our favorite people. When I said good-bye to the Boom Chicago staff, they offered me a part-time job to stay on as their marketing manager. Dave nudged me to consider it, but I wouldn't budge.

"Babe, it's only part time, and I doubt we'd even get past the visa issues. It's time to go home," and then I rubbed his back for comfort.

I stuck with Muay Thai. When I revealed to my kickboxing friend Kim that I was a little scared to go back in because of the hits I took, she said, "I will protect you. We take little steps, OK?" After a little while, I forgot my fear again. During the last class, I told a stocky Asian woman that I was leaving to return to the states. I had never talked to this woman, didn't even know her name, but we sparred together regularly because we had a rhythm like a harmony, so it would feel weird not to say good-bye. She had a wicked left hook, which she landed on my upper arm with painful frequency.

"Shit!" she said after I told her, and she stopped hitting me for a minute. "I'm gonna miss you, man!" And then she pulled back that arm.

Dave and I walked around a lot that last week, waxing nostalgic on the places and experiences that formed our seven-month bubble of an existence.

"Back to real life now?" I asked him, my head on his shoulder looking up at his face.

I thought he might cry.

EPILOGUE: SEPARATION, TO SAVE THE MARRIAGE

If you followed this story from the beginning you might think I got a happy ending. Young girl full of spunk draws some porn, eats some cat food, *almost* marries Jon Bon Jovi, *actually* marries the wrong guy, plunges downward for a while, reemerges better/stronger, meets the love of her life and elopes in Italy! The fairytale, right? Wrong.

Guess what princess, happy endings are hard to come by.

In early 2011 I was sitting in my marriage counselor's office waiting for Dave to arrive. I planned on telling him that we were going to separate, effective immediately. That I was leaving after the session to stay with my sister for a week and that he needed to find a new place to live. All I felt as I waited was heaviness—heavy weariness and heavy sadness. *How did we get here?*

When we returned from Europe, we returned to our old jobs: me to consulting and him to bartending. Only for Dave time away did not make his heart grow fonder. He didn't realize how much he hated the crowds of young drunks and the late hours and the hassle of scheduling time off until he had been away from it for a while. Within four months, he was gone.

Now if there's one thing I stand for it is the pursuit of happiness. It drives everything I do. What the fuck is it all for if not to be happy? And so I supported him as he went to find his. But what do people do if they don't know what that is? Where does a person start?

In Dave's case, he shuffled around, trying out new professions by way of process of elimination. "Nine-to-five desk jobs just aren't for me," he'd say and move toward another path. He always worked, always contributed, just not as much as he wanted, and at amounts that were inconsistent, which made him feel "less than."

Meanwhile, I became the breadwinner, the "stable" one, the one who kept us in health insurance. I went all in with my job, working seventy hours a week. First, it was to prove myself invaluable so that I wouldn't get cut as clients' budgets began to shrink. Then seventy hours became the norm, the expectation. I guess I wanted something tangible as a reward for "my sacrifice," so we bought a house, which only increased our bills, the pressure, and the disparity in our contributions. I was growing resentful and feeling sorry for myself (Where's **my** opportunity to figure out my life? Where's my Rumspringa?). We began doing more and more things apart.

In the beginning, we didn't communicate clearly or directly about what was happening or how we were feeling, choosing instead to sweep it under the rug. I'd reach a point of saturation—a point where I couldn't work another night until nine and then get back up at 6:00 a.m. to do it all over again, including on weekends, all while trying to be a good wife, a good daughter/sister/friend, take care of myself, get groceries, pay bills, and so on. When I felt this way, I would cry. And not just a little bit, but a full-on sob fest that came on strong and lasted for ten minutes, like a summer storm.

When Dave was present for these, he'd feel helpless and go internal. Figuring he was to blame for my state, but also feeling like he had no control, he let chaos rule his response. Wielding its lasso, chaos would ring the noose around his neck and lead him to our home office. There, he'd sit angrily at his computer and mass apply to jobs—regardless of fit—just to take action, any action, that could possibly get him employed, get us back on track.

I let chaos rule my response too. I didn't like being left a sobbing mess. I didn't like that *my* being upset turned into *him* being upset. I didn't like that we moved from taking care of me to taking care of him, but as a problem-solver, I'd go right into that mode, chasing him upstairs and hovering.

"Why are *you* upset?"

"Because I hate this! I don't want you to have to work so much!"

"Yeah, I know," I said, standing behind him, looking at his applications. "But do you really think you'd be happy doing data entry? You've already tried that, and you said you didn't like being in an office…"

"Well, I don't have many choices, do I?"

When we were calm, we could talk about things more rationally. I'd try to provide idealistic advice: "You have a degree, you have experience, you just need to apply for things you're interested in, network, do some informational interviews. It's a number game!" This would go OK for a few minutes until we went into what is arguably the least sexy dynamic in a marriage: parent/kid.

"What jobs did you apply for today?" I asked one night after work while I changed into pajamas and logged back in again. "Weren't you supposed to do the dishes?"

He looked at me, resentful, doing his best to hold back the most epic eye roll. "I don't think you understand what it's like out there, Jen. It's not easy for me like it is for you."

"You think what I'm doing is *easy*? You think I'd be doing this if I had a choice?" It got to the point where we were saying the things we thought were firmly lodged in the Never-Say-That Zone. "God, you know what?" I spit. "You're supposed to make my life easier, but you only make it *harder.*"

He looked at me, sad. "You should have married someone better."

My heart broke. This was my sweetheart, my love. I never wanted him to feel that way. It also broke my heart because sometimes, fleetingly, I thought that too. I put my arms around him. "Don't say that," I soothed. "Never say that."

When these fights came up just once or twice per year, it was easier to pretend we could live like that infinitum. But as they increased in both frequency and emotion, we found ourselves often exhausted and raw. I lived in a perpetual state of anxiety in my own home. *What type of mood will Dave be in? Will I be able to concentrate enough to get my work done tonight? What if I'm not, and I lose my job, and then we lose the house? AHHHHH!* And always in the background: *where is my happiness?*

The first session with our counselor was all about how we communicate.

"So when you're in a bad mood, how do you want Jen to react?" she asked Dave.

"I just need five minutes to shake it off, and then I can talk."

"Did you hear that, Jen? Do you think you can just give him space?"

"Yes."

"And what do you want Dave to do when you cry?"

"I just want him to understand that this is the way I manage stress. I have a good cry, and then it's gone."

"Dave, do you understand that this is just Jen's process for releasing stress?"

"Yes."

Therapists sometimes talk to you like you're a child, but I liked it. We trusted her and saw her over a period of four years and felt good about the fact that we were seeking help before it became irreparable. Every session gave our marriage a good "therapy bump." Before we reverted back to old patterns, that is.

In June of 2010, I left my job to freelance so I could devote more time to my creative pursuits. This was something I had wanted for a long time—something I planned for and saved for (I could safely pay the bills for a year and had lined up work in the meantime). While working from home, I could see Dave's funk in full effect. He was sleeping a lot and moody. We fought. Almost every other day. Again, I couldn't concentrate. The happiness I eked out of my new work/life balance was squashed by the tension in my home.

Whenever I'm facing a major life change, I ask myself the same question: what will make me happier—staying in the situation or heading into the unknown? When the answer comes back as the latter, repeatedly, then I know I'm ready for the change. As our fighting increased, the unknown became less scary.

One night I sat alone in my backyard. Dave had gone back to bartending, so I had nights to myself a few times per week. I just sat quietly and thought about how I'd tell Dave I wanted to separate—that we had tried working on our marriage for several years while living together, but it felt like we were having the same conversation over and over—even with our therapist—and none of it was helping. In fact, it was getting worse. At the very least, a separation would help us clear our heads and give us a respite from all the fighting.

But I was afraid to tell him and didn't know why. It wasn't because I was afraid to have a tough conversation. We'd had plenty of those, even conceding that if things didn't get better one of us was going to have an affair or move out—truths that left us both wincing. So what was I afraid of? Divorce? No, I'd gone through that. Being alone? No. Finally, it came to me: I was afraid he wouldn't do the work, afraid we'd separate for a couple weeks and then he'd "give up." *What if he doesn't fight for me?*

Well, you want him to fight for you. What does that tell you? And then the words became clear. The next evening, I found him lying in our bed. I sat down next to him, stroked his face, his neck. "My sweetheart…" I began, my voice a little shaky but resigned. I told him what was in my heart. I told him I wanted to separate as a means to save the marriage and that I believed we could. That the space would do us good. He heard me, even thanked me for being brave enough to start the *real* conversation. But he did not want a physical separation and wrote me a contract detailing specific actions he would take to win my trust and eliminate the tension in our home.

Should I give him one more chance?

"OK, as long as you do those things, you can stay."

So when he stopped doing some of those things—things that he himself outlined without any prompting—I called him out on it, which made him defensive and me angry. And that's when I made

our last appointment with our therapist that day. It shocked Dave—
to have this "sprung" on him—but I told him it was nonnegotiable,
and to his credit he adjusted to this new reality rather quickly. This
allowed us to use the rest of the session to talk about our feelings
surrounding it and the terms.

"I'm afraid you're just trying to get me out of the house so you can
divorce me."

"No way," I said. "You do the work, and I've got you. I want you
back with me."

We came up with The Rules of Separation:
1. No dating (read: fucking) other people
2. Talk every day
3. Do the work

That first couple of weeks sucked. It took him about that long to
trust me when I said fixing the marriage was the goal, but once he
did, it was full speed ahead. We had the best conversations of our
marriage. We were vulnerable with each other, and we were also
each other's protectors. We went on dates. I was able to concentrate on my work, and he was able to figure out his path. And now?
Now he's back home with me. Now he makes my life easier *and*
happier. Now *he* picks up the health insurance.

It's quite a powerful feeling to separate and come back together. It
makes clear you're both there by choice versus obligation, which
makes it easier to be vulnerable with each other because we know
we have each other's back. It made us *partners*. While we didn't
make a full 180-degree turn from where we were, I can say with
confidence we made a solid 165.

What do you know, princess? You got your happy ending after all.

AFTERWORD: YOU'RE NOT PRETTY ENOUGH, THE MOVEMENT

In 2010, I began telling my stories live onstage in DC and New York City. The one that resonated with people the most was the story about my former marriage and divorce. *Especially* the comments my ex-husband made about me not being "pretty enough." It tapped into something. When I launched a website to promote my writing and performances, I used that phrase, *you're not pretty enough*, as the domain name. I thought it was catchy, but I also thought it was a "joke" only my friends and family would catch, and maybe a few others.

And then something interesting happened. I noticed I got a startling amount of traffic from people who Googled some variation of the phrase "what to do when you're not pretty" or "how to be pretty when you're not?"

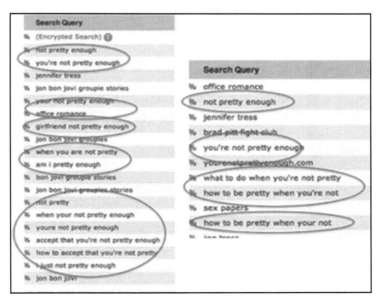

It surprised me, seeing all these searches. At first I thought, *Why are people asking the Internet?* To me, it's the same as asking a Magic 8-Ball. What answer could possibly satisfy that question? And yet, my site was among the first to come up. Being what it was at that time, I'm sure those anonymous web searchers thought, *Who in the hell is Jen Tress?* And, *does Jon Bon Jovi have a restraining order?*

Month after month I'd see these key words, that phrase, in my analytics. It bothered me of course, but I didn't know how to respond. Hell, I didn't know if I *should* respond. Then I heard about a trend of tweens and teens uploading videos to YouTube and asking the Internet, again, to judge whether or not they were ugly. Some of the comments were encouraging or suggestive: "ur pretty, you should just get bangs, yo!" But many were unnecessarily cruel. That's what motivated me to take action. But where to start?

I went into consultant mode. What did I want to put out there? What was my vision, so to speak? That came fairly easy: I wanted to provide an alternative to the current environment. I wanted there to be a safe online space where people, mostly females I assumed, could explore that "not pretty enough" feeling in a way that was authentic, empowered, and productive. I wanted it to be a place to have a conversation or a good think versus a five-second sound bite, good or bad. Those inspirational messages we see—"You ARE beautiful"—those are good reminders. But are they enough to change our perspective and behaviors in a permanent way?

Knowing my perspective alone wouldn't nearly answer that "Am I pretty enough?" question, I sought out other voices. I collaborated with universities in the metro Washington, DC area, with women and gender studies departments and faculty and students. I set up on campuses and administered hundreds of surveys around this feeling, asking, "When was the last time you felt 'not pretty enough?' What drove that feeling? How did/do you pull yourself out of it? What advice would you give to others who feel this way?"

I developed a web series modeled after Dan Savage's **It Gets Better Project** and watched, fascinated, as the subjects I interviewed came to some serious revelations. One woman said to me, "What I discovered about myself, talking through this, literally changed my life." Everyone's story is different. We each enter that "not pretty enough" feeling via our unique experiences, which are influenced by culture, class, race, sexuality, and gender, among other factors. But even through our differences, some common themes emerged.

1. **It's all about feeling "enough." "Pretty" is just the gateway word.** No matter what descriptor you put in front of that word *enough*, be it pretty, or smart, or more generally, good, it all boils down to feeling like we are not "enough." Pretty is an easy filler because looks are the easiest (and laziest) things to judge, to categorize, especially in Western culture where beauty is prized and norms are held up to unachievable standards.

2. **Parents set the tone.** They—or whoever our caretakers are as we grow from childhood into adulthood—are the ones who teach us the way. Even if our parents love us and tell us we're beautiful, we still pick up their habits. If parents are focused on their own appearance in a way that is out of balance with all other parts of their identity, chances are their children will internalize that. If parents validate and guide their children based on the particular needs and interests of the child, then that, unsurprisingly, has a really positive affect. The big rub is this: parents become the template for the types of relationships we choose throughout our lives, whether they be romantic or with friends.

3. **Remove toxic people from your life.** If you're not getting what you need from your direct support network or if some of your primary relationships make you feel bad about yourself or not accepted, then it's time to move on. Easier said than done though, right? But remember: as an adult, you have options. You don't *have* to remain friends with people or continue dating someone who doesn't make you happy. You don't have to officially "break up" with them either—especially friends or even parents, but you can set boundaries.

4. **There are short-term fixes.** And this may surprise you, but some people really don't think about it. For those of us who do, that "not pretty enough" feeling is more of a passing thought— something that comes up as we're getting ready or if we're out with "prettier" people with whom we compare ourselves. That's normal and can be pushed aside with some easy tactics. The site contains lots of tips and tools for how to do this, including great insights from video contributors.

5. **Longer term, we're all works in progress.** When those short-term fixes don't work, it's time to pull in your "helpers," the people in your life who listen and lift you up, people you can open up to and who make you feel safe. The ultimate goal is self-acceptance, but as one of the video contributors said, "You always hear, 'Love yourself.' Well, shit, if it were that easy, we'd all be doing that, wouldn't we?" Indeed. Self-acceptance doesn't mean you give yourself a free pass if you genuinely make a mistake. It means you can assess yourself accurately and accept who you are. Sometimes we can't do that for ourselves. Sometimes we need help from our family and friends and significant others and sometimes from professionals.

6. **There is no one ideal of beauty.** Even with the standards put out there through the media, let me tell you that people of all types

are hooking up. Everywhere. All the time. And I know that once I'm in someone's company for more than ten seconds, I'm past the physical. If you're nice, I like you. If you're funny, I like you. If you have a curious intellect, I like you. If you like to drink cocktails and talk in funny voices, I like you. If you get the point of this paragraph, I like you.

So where does this leave me? What are my own feelings about being "pretty enough" given my story? When people hear or read my "not pretty enough" story, they often say to me, "how could anyone ever say that to *you?*" Well, guess what? Even "pretty" girls feel unpretty. Even "pretty" girls get told that. How many stories from actresses and models have we heard where they were told, "if you just lost 10 pounds…"

For me, my "prettiness" was always wrapped up in my weight as well. I knew I had some assets: a pretty face, some serious hair, and a proportional T&A body. I like to put it away, with food and drink, and as someone who does not pay a lot of attention to the scale I can easily put on 10 pounds in a snap. Sometimes 20. Sometimes 40. I must have destroyed all of my "fat" photos. I wouldn't be ashamed of them now, nor would I be ashamed of my body. But back then – when I was less mature, when I didn't know or accept myself as well as I do know – if I saw a "fat" photo, I'd trash it.

Growing up, my friends and family treated me the same, loved me the same no matter my size. But it was different with the boys. I noticed that when I was skinnier, I didn't get called a fat ass. I noticed I got more positive attention.

And I used that positive attention as a corollary to positive things. I got that promotion or that guy because I was "skinny," or I didn't because I was "fat." It took some time for me to understand that kind of thinking wasn't going to get me anywhere. It took me some time to figure out that wasn't true. I still have those "not pretty enough" feelings, but they're only little wisps of things, like a gnat I can swat away. I think this will remain the status quo.

I think, finally, I'm enough.

ACKNOWLEDGEMENTS

There are so many people to thank! To name them all individually would do injustice to others I'd undoubtedly forget, so I'll limit it to a few who were instrumental.

To Tara Susman-Peña, thank you for making me feel like I had something to say (and that others would want to hear it) during our early writing sessions. To Claire Ruppert (and the Emerson Writers Workshop in DC), thank you for forcing me to really home in on the themes that were important and for helping me realize my writer's voice. To Shawna Kenney and Cara Bruce for your invaluable feedback and editing notes. It was through you that I first felt I was getting somewhere. To Susan Kittenplan, Jennie Willink and Ian Fay for guiding me in the right direction when I wanted to go bigger. To Jaime Windon (The Blonde Photographer) for seeing my sassy and raising it as evidenced by her amazing shots. To Wendy Stamberger, my good friend since third grade (as she said, "I *knew* that girl with the eyebrows") and a major talent in the design world, for her artistic and personal support. Whenever I needed it. In perpetuity.

To the Washington DC and NYC storytelling communities. Some of my favorite people are in this community, which I find so supportive and inspiring. Telling these stories on stage gave me keen insight into what was working and what wasn't. And to the fans and supporters of storytelling: I want to nuzzle you in my ample bosom! You are a warm bunch. When I first started out I thought I would puke and had to pee every 5 minutes before a performance. Now I can't wait to get out there.

To my friends who read early drafts and came to watch me perform. Thank you for the honest, super helpful feedback while also being super encouraging. You were always my target audience.

To my dad for being such a loving, caring goofball of a guy and for tolerating me renting *Girls Just Want to Have Fun* every other weekend for like, two years. To my stepmom Vicki for taking on this crazy little trio and embracing us fully. You're my buddies. To my mom for being a model in countless ways, I'm not even sure I've fully absorbed it. To my sister, Rebecca, for never ever judging me and supporting me all of the time. You're my go to in many, many situations. Also you think I'm the funniest and when we get rolling it sounds like a dolphin and a machine gun are mating. And *that's* the funniest. To my sister's wife Erin (sissy two); your wonderful, pure spirit is such a gift. To my in-laws for always treating me like their daughter/ sister/aunt. Thank you for your unwavering support.

To my husband Dave for walking through all the muck with me. Life can be a real shit show but you give me the most comfort. I can't wait for more adventures with you. Team Tress: clear eyes, full hearts, can't lose.

3776164R00110

Made in the USA
San Bernardino, CA
20 August 2013